## Praise for *Inspired by Fear*

"Kris Jennings weaves together vivid storytelling with concrete tools to show us how to work with (not against) fear. If you're leading change of any kind, you'll want to read this book." —Kristen Lisanti, founder of Radiant Change

"This book succinctly captures what it took me decades to learn about change as an HR professional and leader. The stories accurately depict the rollercoaster of large-scale change and the emotions of people on it. I wish I'd had it in grad school as a quick read that is both thoughtful and theoretical like John Kotter and William Bridges, and deep and powerful emotionally like Brené Brown. Even now as I launch into new endeavors, I use the distilled wisdom of 'Getting better at leading change requires exploring fear in yourself and your team.'" —Monica Smith, small business entrepreneur and founder, Mint Canary LLC

"Refreshingly honest and practical, leaders will frequently reference this book for the memorable stories and the proven techniques. By the end, it feels like you've already got a better idea of what's coming and more confidence to lead through it." —Sarah Strehl, chief human resources officer, ECMC Group

"*Inspired by Fear* belongs in the same collection as *The Five Dysfunctions of a Team* and other great Leadership Fables. It's easy to read, engaging, and powerful. Leaders and change managers alike will reap the benefits of this compelling and practical guide. It is a must-read. From the boardroom to 1:1 feedback moments, this book contains perspectives and tools leaders across sectors can equip themselves with to become more empathetic leaders, improve emotional intelligence, and lead teams successfully through change." —Chrystal Checketts, leadership consultant and executive coach

"*Inspired by Fear* will feel like you are reading your own thoughts and feelings about change management. This book will provide you with the tools and insight to approach change not only in your work life, but your personal life too!"

—Jill Claggett,
30-year HR professional

"*Inspired by Fear* provides leaders with a guidebook to address one of the most overlooked aspects of leading change – emotions. So often, we hear about the "practical" and the "emotional" as if they are separate entities. Kris Jennings shows us they are one and the same. She provides leaders with concrete actions to acknowledge the fear, anxiety, anger, and wide variety of emotions that arise during change and inspires people to act *with* their emotions. Highly recommend it to anyone leading change, big or small!"

—Heather Whelpley,
keynote speaker and award-winning author of
*An Overachiever's Guide to Breaking the Rules* and *Grounded Wildness*

"If you feel uncertain about what you're supposed to do in an ever-changing business environment, this is a book you want on your desk. Kris Jennings uses storytelling and everyday examples to break down complex topics that arm you with tools and real-world advice."

—Kristi Norton,
vice president, UnitedHealth Group Strategy

"*Inspired by Fear* is an essential playbook for anyone leading change, offering practical tools and strategies to navigate the human side of transformation. With actionable techniques to help people transition from fear and uncertainty to acceptance and confidence, Jennings equips leaders with the capacity to develop their own and their team's long-term ability to successfully navigate change. A must-read I wish I'd had earlier in my career!"

—Sarah Moran,
strategic leadership and development consultant

"Having worked with her on two large change efforts, I can tell you Jennings' focus on human fear and emotions during major change works! You'll refer to this book often."
—Cathie Mayr,
retired partner, Ernst & Young

"Going through change can be difficult. Jennings reminds us of the importance of human connection and being intentional in interactions. *Inspired by Fear* quickly reveals itself to be a profound exploration of how we can enrich our lives by focusing on the people around us and helping them navigate change. Every change practitioner should read this annually to remind themself of the power you can unleash in human potential."
—Gus Broman,
change consultant, adjunct professor,
and author of *Bridge to Teen*

"Many underestimate the impact fear can have on our daily lives, let alone a managing a team through critical change event. Kris Jennings does a masterful job presenting simple, rational methods and techniques that will help you be a successful Change Leader . . . not only in the workplace, but in your personal life as well. An invaluable read!"
—Brett Tibbs,
principal, Arches Consulting LLC

"A wise leader knows that focusing on people is what makes change successful. This book is packed with ideas on how to make change simpler and easier."
—Teresa Sande,
consultant, coach, and author of *Find Your Fierce*

# INSPIRED — BY — FEAR

**BECOMING A COURAGEOUS
CHANGE LEADER**

KRIS JENNINGS

Inspired by Fear: Becoming a Courageous Change Leader
Copyright © 2024 by Kris Jennings

All rights reserved. No portion of this book may be reproduced in any form without written permission in writing from the author, except as permitted by U.S. copyright law.

This publication is designed to provide accurate and authoritative information in regard to the subject matter covered. While the author has used their best efforts in preparing this book, they make no representations or warranties with respect to the accuracy or completeness of the contents of this book and specifically disclaim any implied warranties of merchantability or fitness for a particular purpose. No warranty may be created or extended by sales representatives or written sales materials. The advice and strategies contained herein may not be suitable for your situation. You should consult with a professional when appropriate. The author shall not be liable for any loss of profit or any other commercial damages, including but not limited to special, incidental, consequential, personal, or other damages.

ISBN: 979-8-9913865-1-7

Library of Congress Control Number: 2024917501

Book Cover and Interior Design by Rachel Valliere | Printed Page Studios

Author Photo by Lucas Botz | Botz Photography

First Edition
Published by Kris Jennings
Minneapolis, Minnesota
https://krisjennings.com

*For those doing the hard thing, despite fear's presence.*

*Courage is not the absence of fear, but rather the assessment that something else is more important than fear.*
— Franklin D. Roosevelt

# Contents

**Introduction**   xv
The Power of Fear   xvii
How This Book Can Help You   xviii

**A Manifesto for Leaders During Change**   xxi

**1: Leading People Through Change**   1
*Your Response to Fear Matters to Your Team*

Choosing Your Response to Fear   3
Noticing the Physical Sensations of Fear   5
Naming the Fear   7
Nudging a Mindset Shift   10
Designing Courage One Shift at a Time   11
Cera Day's Story   13
One Small Shift: Nudging Your Response   15
Putting It Into Practice *free mini-course and downloadable tool kit*   17

**2: What If I Fail?**   19
*Choosing the Hero's Journey*

Becoming the Hero   21
Identifying Advisers for Your Adventure   24
Hearing How the Story Ends   26

| | |
|---|---|
| Working Toward "Something Better" | 28 |
| Setting Expectations for Reaching "Something Better" | 30 |
| Cera Day's Story | 34 |
| One Small Shift: Heroes Ask for Help | 37 |

## 3: Is Anything in My Control?    39
*Choosing to Influence Rather Than Micromanage*

| | |
|---|---|
| Recognizing Areas of Influence | 41 |
| Creating the Environment | 43 |
| Presenting Choices and Understanding Nudges | 45 |
| Rewarding Choices and Using Encouraging Language | 47 |
| Cera Day's Story | 49 |
| One Small Shift: Influencing Choices | 51 |

## 4: Why Are We Doing This?    53
*Developing Your People*

| | |
|---|---|
| Leading People versus Managing Tasks | 56 |
| Answering the Question of *Why* | 60 |
| Managing the Process (Your Project Manager) | 61 |
| Developing and Influencing People (Your Business Change Lead) | 64 |
| Cera Day's Story | 65 |
| One Small Shift: A Why That's More Powerful Than Fear | 68 |

## 5: Am I Strong Enough?    71
*Managing Your Energy*

| | |
|---|---|
| A Note from the Author | 71 |
| Notice Sensations Using Body Scanning | 72 |
| Releasing Stress Through Breathwork | 74 |
| Getting Outside | 74 |
| One Small Shift: Preventing Burnout through Mindfulness | 76 |

## 6: What's Next on This Emotional Roller Coaster?     79
*Influencing People*

| | |
|---|---|
| Accepting Emotions | 80 |
| Anticipating Emotions | 83 |
| Using the 3N Influencing Technique | 86 |
| Influencing Your Boss Out of Fear | 88 |
| Influencing a Peer Who's Angry | 90 |
| Influencing a Team Member Who's Sad | 94 |
| Influencing for Outcomes | 97 |
| Cera Day's Story | 97 |
| One Small Shift: Accepting Emotions to Influence Behaviors | 100 |

## 7: Is Anyone Listening?     103
*Building Relationships Through Conversations*

| | |
|---|---|
| Cultivating Conversations | 104 |
| Amplifying Pleasant Emotions | 106 |
| Asking Great Questions | 108 |
| Listening and Responding | 109 |
| Inviting Others into the Conversation | 110 |
| Cera Day's Story | 112 |
| One Small Shift: Conversing *with* People | 115 |

## 8: Can We Learn It in Time?     117
*Learning by Doing*

| | |
|---|---|
| Learning Along the Way | 119 |
| Involving Others as Part of Their Learning | 121 |
| Embedding Teachers in Your Team | 123 |
| Formalizing Knowledge Transfer | 125 |
| Measuring Learning Progress | 126 |
| Cera Day's Story | 128 |
| One Small Shift: Learning by Doing | 130 |

## 9: Is It Ever Going to End? — **133**
*Rewarding Change*

| | |
|---|---|
| Completing the Transition | 134 |
| Emphasizing the Upside | 137 |
| Making Change Fun | 139 |
| Rewarding Change | 140 |
| Rooting Out Resistance | 143 |
| Continuing Improvement | 146 |
| Cera Day's Story | 147 |
| One Small Shift: Celebrating Growth | 150 |

## 10: Courageous Change Leadership — **153**
*Putting People First*

| | |
|---|---|
| One Small Shift: Inspiring Courage | 161 |

## Bibliography — **163**

## Acknowledgments — **167**

# List of Figures

*Figure 1*
**Slowing Down Fear Reactions**     22

*Figure 2*
**Circles of Influence Model**     42

*Figure 3*
**Human-Centered Change Model**     58

*Figure 4*
**Emotional Checkmark Change Journey**     85

*Figure 5*
**Emotion-driven Conversations**     106

*Figure 6*
**Rewarding Change Model**     141

# Introduction

It's happening. You've been thrust into a high-stakes leadership situation. Maybe you saw it on the horizon and braced yourself, or perhaps it caught you off guard. Either way, your current reality is volatile, uncertain, complex, and ambiguous. It's also known as change.

You must lead a team through this change, an experience that will shift so often that it will be hard to describe. You're excited about the future, but your experience predicts that getting there won't be easy. You've already felt some bumps, and more are surely coming. You want to rise to the opportunity, yet doubt, angst, and trepidation permeate your feelings.

If you're willing to admit it, fear is the strongest emotion you may be experiencing right now. So, how will you get through it all?

Getting through the transition starts with emotions. Learning how to accept fear, frustration, and grief is part of what you need to do as a courageous change leader. You and your team will feel a wide range of emotions. Attempting to skip over them means getting stuck in reactive behavior loops of resistance. Yet most of us have been conditioned to do just that, especially at work. Many of us also lack the skills to talk about "unpleasant" feelings. Getting better at leading change requires exploring fear in yourself and your team. It also means learning how to talk about it.

For the sake of efficiency, organizations have attempted to control change using highly structured approaches involving intricate sets of tasks and activities. Those activities typically downplay human emotions and focus on the logical reasons for change, sharing loads of information and prescriptive step-by-step training instructions. These well-intentioned efforts to manage change often leave out important motivational elements. People are not solely rational. They are, however, predictable. Particularly when it comes to anticipating and creating fear through stories based on past personal experiences. Those stories impact how they behave during change.

This book, *Inspired by Fear*, invites you to consider a more human-centered approach to organizational change that factors emotions into the equation. One that starts with a single change leader who believes in nurturing relationships to build loyalty and develop people. This is playing the long game of growth. Ironically, it leads to better results faster (as tested during my two decades of applying these concepts in global organizations experiencing transformational change). This book provides a missing layer of context around human motivation and emotions that helps leaders understand the connection with behavior change.

The cornerstone principle of this approach is that emotions influence behaviors. How you *feel* influences what you *do*. It stands to reason that if we want to change behaviors, we must first learn to influence emotions. But this is no small feat for leaders, who face the challenge of managing their emotions to quickly adjust their own behaviors while simultaneously applying this principle to influence their teams and other important stakeholders. It requires focus on two fronts, which isn't easy to do. But if you can master this principle—starting with reframing fear—the impact becomes exponential for you, your team, and your organization.

## The Power of Fear

It's hard to do anything during change if you cannot shift yourself or your team out of paralyzing fear. You cannot learn, and you cannot collaboratively problem-solve when scared. That's the crux of what you're learning to do as you accept fear and choose to proceed anyway in the true sense of courage. It's uncomfortable, yet everything you want for yourself and your team is on the other side of fear. Like all emotions, fear is a social construct used to create meaning among people. You may already be creating meaning in your mind by anticipating how hard it will be or using words that paint a picture of an impossible task. Many of us amplify fear's power inadvertently, which makes change even more difficult.

My understanding of the power of fear to prevent us from getting what we want comes from both professional and personal wisdom. During the COVID-19 pandemic, like many other people, I experienced pervasive fear that looked like repetitive gloom-and-doom loops and a host of physical and emotional symptoms. I sought help from a therapist who diagnosed me with chronic post-traumatic stress disorder (PTSD). To be clear, trauma is an event, while fear is a response to that event. Only a small percentage of people who experience trauma will go on to develop the disordered response that is full PTSD. For me, that looked like getting stuck in a fear reaction. In addition to specific therapy modalities, I sought to redesign behaviors in my life to shift this automatic reaction into a conscious response. I started by noticing what I was doing and then reflected backward to recognize the unpleasant feelings that led to those coping behaviors.

Eventually, I learned to slow everything down to practice new, healthier behaviors. I used physical sensations to help me pause before reacting. I realized I could redefine those sensations by changing my thought patterns. "I'm terrified that something bad will happen, so I've got to do something right now" became "I'm safe, and I can take all the time I need to figure this out." My relationships changed as I stopped reacting and started responding. I also saw the gift in my fear that could help others. The fear wasn't gone, but I learned how to accept it. I redefined fear as something that meant an opportunity for growth rather than a limit in my life. I owned the fear and chose how to respond.

## How This Book Can Help You

Reframing fear allows you to direct your energy toward other leadership behaviors. While fear is the spark point to help you recognize potential growth moments during change, this book helps leaders *behave* differently by:

- Using emotions to influence behaviors
- Developing allies to help you influence others
- Engaging people through ongoing conversations
- Maximizing learning by doing
- Rewarding change to encourage more of it

## Introduction

*Inspired by Fear* walks you through making small shifts to quickly become a better change leader. It starts by helping yourself predict success when your fear suggests failure. You'll see what good change leadership looks and feels like through the perspective of Cera Day, a composite character drawn from hundreds of change leaders I've coached. She learns how to become a more courageous change leader during a once-in-a-career project she's been asked to sponsor. She experiences many variations of fear, including panic, apprehension, overwhelm, anxiety, worry, and doubt.

Each chapter addresses a specific fear and practical guidance to help you make small shifts *while* leading. Becoming a courageous change leader happens through behaviors repeated consistently over time. The concepts, models, and techniques shared in the book are supplemented with a free online mini-course and downloadable tool kit that helps you put them into action. (See the instructions at the end of chapter 1.)

Change doesn't have to be all unpleasant, nor does fear. It's possible to redefine it and cultivate more pleasant emotions like joy, curiosity, playfulness, hope, gratitude, and appreciation. Those positive feelings pull people into doing things they didn't think possible.

Fear can become courage. I know because I've lived it.

# A Manifesto for Leaders During Change

Accept fear; it's human.

Heroes find masters to learn from.

You cannot control everything, but you can influence a lot.

People influence people.

People remember how you made them feel.

Emotions influence behaviors.

Conversations build teams.

Learn as you go.

The best rewards are fast, easy, and free.

Courage is a single step; serving others is more important than fear.

# Accept Fear; It's Human

# 1

# LEADING PEOPLE THROUGH CHANGE

*Your Response to Fear Matters to Your Team*

*Click. Click. Click.*

Cera Day fidgets mindlessly with her retractable ballpoint pen while waiting in her office. Only the glow of her laptop lights the room this early in the day. Her closed door signals to her team that she doesn't want to be disturbed. Not now, anyway. Her boss and the organization's chief executive officer, Sophia, will return from the board meeting any minute. Today, they're reviewing funding requirements for a program that could change Cera's work world.

Cera wants this. It's long overdue. Her team's work methods need an upgrade, as they've been trying to "make do" for over a decade. She's made the same request to upgrade her team's technology for nearly five years. Without the right tools, her Operations team has been unable to provide the business with insights on people trends, such as which managers have the highest turnover and how long it takes to staff a position. Finally, it got painful enough last year with an acquisition that doubled the organization. Leaders would ask basic questions such as, "How many employees versus contractors do we have?" When Cera couldn't answer them quickly or with certainty, it invariably prompted the question, "Why not?"

Because of its rapid growth, the organization needs common technology and processes for its back-office functions. This creates operational efficiency, including quick reporting to make critical decisions, such as how many open positions can be trimmed to manage forecasted expenses. The pain point Cera has been experiencing for years got real to her leadership after the acquisition.

A sharp knock at the door startles Cera out of her reverie. "Do you have a minute?" Sophia asks as she walks into the office.

"Of course," Cera says. "How'd it go?"

"It's a go. Now the real work begins."

Cera exhales. It takes a minute for the news to sink in. She has learned how to make do while the business invested capital in other customer-facing improvements and new products. She gets that. But it's left her in the position of playing catch-up. This will change that. Instead of operating like order-takers, they'll finally have a chance to anticipate issues and influence strategically using the on-demand analytics of a single system for the entire workforce.

Cera pauses. She's had much time to prepare for this moment. She has a plan that covers most of the how; that doesn't scare her. She's managed plenty of complicated projects.

It's the people side that she needs to figure out.

Cera has never done anything that will have such a broad impact on the organization, from the executive team to frontline workers—and, of course, for her and her team. It's massive.

On top of that, Cera will be front and center as her team, peers, and project team members look to her for guidance in making decisions that will impact the business for decades. She won't get another chance like this again soon—or maybe ever—in her career. It's a tremendous leadership opportunity.

The weight hits her as she recognizes that success rests with her. Yet who's going to help her? How will she handle this stress—and the stress it will put on her team?

Cera doesn't like the way that makes her feel: *afraid*. So she pushes the feelings and tension in her body aside and does what she knows best: digging into the details of organizing the work. She'll deal with emotions and people later.

## Choosing Your Response to Fear

Getting tapped to lead a significant change can bring up feelings of fear. You find yourself suddenly in the spotlight and with an enormous amount of additional work, sorting through tasks you've never done before that have substantial long-term implications for your team and your organization. Your change may be:

- A new technology that's modernizing or significantly advancing your team's capabilities
- An organization-wide strategic growth initiative that you own
- An acquisition that significantly increased your organization's size and has left you with disparate processes, technology, and people to synthesize
- A reorganization that may involve new

responsibilities and team members that need to figure out how to work together
- Changing how work gets done across your team to do more, faster, or better

In any of these scenarios, you've got to get up to speed on leading change fast. But what does "good" change leadership look like? Can't you outsource this by hiring an expert? Or delegate it to one of your managers? Isn't it good enough to use the change tool kit and templates provided to you?

It's scary, particularly when you recognize how you lead will significantly impact others during and long after the experience. Keeping that long-term perspective is a north star to guide you throughout your change. What you say and do will leave an impression on your team long after the experts leave, far more deeply than whether you use the "right" tools. It's about using relationships that already exist and that will flourish well beyond the end date to help the next change go even faster and more smoothly.

But before you can get there, let's explore fear and how it might hold you back from reaching that goal. Something unfamiliar like change can send our minds into protective prediction mode, filling in gaps and creating stories based on past experiences. All humans do this to protect themselves, yet each of us makes a different prediction based on our life experiences. You can shift a reaction into a more measured, conscious response by better understanding your personal clues that signal fear's presence.

Courage isn't about becoming fearless. It's about noticing and accepting fear as part of being human and then acting despite feeling it. Altruism in service to others is one of the most powerful motivators to overcome fear. In this case, you're moving toward something more important than fear: leading your team through this change. Putting your people first begins with your capability to accept fear and consciously act anyway.

## Noticing the Physical Sensations of Fear

While you may associate fear with something in your mind, it also happens in your body. The physiological purpose of fear is to protect. A burst of cortisol delivers quick energy to the body to evade predators or find extra strength to defend ourselves. In other cases, "playing dead" or appeasing may show up as responses. American counselor and author Pete Walker calls these responses the 4 *F*'s: fight, flight, freeze, or fawn. Humans also experience fear at work, but most of us aren't trained to recognize the 4 *F*'s in ourselves or others. Using the body's physical clues and noticing behaviors can help you do this more quickly.

Let's look at the 4 *F*'s, including the physical sensations and workplace behaviors that may be present to help you notice fear:

| Fear Response | Physical Clues and Behaviors |
| --- | --- |
| **Fight:** Confront the threat (high energy) | • Tight jaw<br>• Grinding teeth<br>• Anger, rage, and confrontation |
| **Flight:** Run away from the threat (high energy) | • Fidgeting, tension, or the feeling of being trapped<br>• Anxiety, panic, or avoidance |

CONTINUED →

| Fear Response | Physical Clues and Behaviors |
|---|---|
| **Freeze:** Shut down to block the threat (low energy) | • Sense of dread<br>• Pale skin<br>• Dissociation, numbness, and the feeling of shutting down |
| **Fawn:** Appease the threat (low energy) | • Agreeableness and people-pleasing<br>• A tendency to be overly helpful<br>• Poor boundaries |

Fear prompts a range of behaviors, both action and inaction. That can make it challenging to recognize. Yet precision isn't important. Simply recognizing that fear may be present helps you pause before deciding what to do. Here are two examples of how fear influences behaviors—both action and inaction—at work:

1. **A compulsive feeling to do something or to do more.** This is often associated with anxiety (e.g., "I'm not getting enough done!") or overwhelmed (e.g., "I have too much to do; I've got to get to the next meeting!"). This may reflect a fight-or-flight fear response.

2. **Procrastination or doing nothing when there's uncertainty.** This includes waiting for directions on what to do or simply complying with instructions. This may reflect a freeze or fawn fear response.

The 4 *F*'s and body sensations can help you notice fear in the moment. Having emotional awareness allows you to pause before responding. In other words, you can consciously respond rather than unconsciously react to fear. During change, using these clues is an underutilized asset because it helps you shift out of fear faster, which ultimately leads to better leadership decisions.

## Naming the Fear

Human emotions are wide-ranging—everything from extreme terror to blissful joy. In 1980, psychologist J. A. Russell found a way to classify them using his circumplex model. Two independent axes evaluate the emotion on a continuum: pleasant-unpleasant and active-inactive levels. This model, along with more recent research on the brain and emotions by neuroscientists, psychologists, and behaviorists, helps us understand how fear influences behavior during change.

As you may have guessed, most of us want to feel pleasant emotions more often and reduce, eliminate, or avoid the unpleasant ones. This is an important factor in change to understand the natural human tendency to avoid fear. It's unpleasant—and the more intense it is, the more actively we avoid it. For example, the time leading up to and immediately following a change is often more intense. Those who haven't prepared may feel panic, which activates resistance to what's being asked of them, such as attending training or beginning to do things differently in their jobs. At the other end of the intensity spectrum is uncertainty. Throughout a change, but particularly at the beginning, apprehension and uncertainty exist. Those forms of fear are more likely to cause inaction, such as ignoring communication or deprioritizing work related to the change. Fear is both constant and predictable during change.

One of the best strategies for reducing fear is improving the **emotional literacy** to talk about it. Naming fear in all its forms helps tame it. In her book *How Emotions Are Made*, Lisa Feldman Barrett debunks the notion that there is a universal way to physically feel or verbally and nonverbally express fear and other emotions. Basically, we all use different words to describe fear and its forms based on what we learned early in life. We were given specific words in specific situations that represent specific feelings. Some caregivers and cultures have more words than others, which means we're coming into work without the tools to understand one another. We're not on the same page about fear and how to talk about the specific way we're feeling.

Having a common language around fear is important so that you and your team members can quickly tell one another what support is needed. The actions to help someone feeling uncertain are quite different from those of someone who's feeling panicked, as the intensity level of what the person feels impacts what they are likely to do.

Change leaders show their team how to ask for help by naming the fear. Team members begin to normalize their experience; and consistent language helps the group remain connected, rather than feeling misunderstood—or, worse, ignored. In the simplest form, this is naming the category: "I feel fear."

The next level of granularity is variations that describe different levels of unpleasantness or activation. These words can help you get more precise with your team about their experience; and when you begin to recognize these words as forms of fear, you'll be in a better position to help yourself and others pause before reacting. Here are some common words people use to describe fear:

| Form of Fear | Description |
|---|---|
| Panic | Terror, dread |
| Anxiety | Persistent worry, concern, racing thoughts |
| Worry | Fretting, stewing, agonizing |
| Overwhelm | Inundated, swamped, defeated, exhausted |
| Apprehension | Uneasiness, trepidation, hesitation |
| Uncertainty | Insecure, self-doubting, timid |

People will use different words—or no words at all—to describe fear. It's less important that you and your team unify your language, and more important that you use the words to open conversations that lead to understanding. Fear's protective purpose can prevent appropriate action. When combined with the body sensations, the words also help bring hidden fear to the surface, which helps you make a conscious choice rather than react. At work, the language and body sensations that serve as clues of fear may look like:

- "I felt *anxious* when presenting to the national sales team. I had difficulty concentrating and bounced from one thought to another. My palms were sweaty, and my heart was racing. I wanted to run out of the room."
- "I feel *worried* about my leadership on this project. I wonder if others are judging me, and I'm reluctant to ask for help."
- "I feel *overwhelmed* by how much work is on my plate. My body feels physically drained, and I have low energy. I feel I don't have a choice."

There are no right or wrong answers to body sensations or language. Every person's response to fear is unique. However, fear responses are built into being human, so noticing and naming it can help us slow down before acting. The more we notice and name what we feel as fear, the less power it has over our actions.

## Nudging a Mindset Shift

Now that we've learned how to use the body's clues to notice fear and created an understanding about the language of fear, let's explore how your mindset fits in.

Our brains are great at pattern recognition. To do that quickly, our mind fills in gaps based on what we think will happen. This isn't always accurate. Sometimes a strong feeling will prompt us to act incorrectly. That's the case when it comes to fear and how it influences your change leadership behaviors. There's a time for thinking fast and, other times, slowing down. The form of fear you feel may be prompting you to act more quickly than what's ideal or avoid action that would be beneficial. Much of that stems from defining fear as unpleasant or "bad." Shifting that mindset requires us to challenge our thinking patterns. We do this by establishing new, positive pathways in our brain through ***neuroplasticity***. The mindset shift we're influencing is that fear is not bad, but rather a fantastically fast and consistent way to recognize growth opportunities.

To understand this mindset shift in action as it relates to change, think back to your first day on the job. Every aspect of a new environment was (mildly) threatening because it was unfamiliar: *How do I badge in? Where's the restroom? How do I* pay at the cafeteria? What should I say during this meeting? Is this peer a potential ally or adversary?

You probably felt as though you were "on" the whole time as your brain continuously assessed each new circumstance to decide what to do. You might not even have noticed at the time that what you were feeling was the category of fear. Learning to recognize new patterns is tiring as our brains work extra hard to predict things. (The same experience happens to kindergartners during the first weeks of school, which is why so many of them need extra naps!) But over time, and with repetition, patterns emerged. Your brain adjusted, fear diminished, and energy was redirected to more important pattern recognition, such as making the most of your new environment, building relationships, and finding new ways to solve problems.

Noticing fear in whatever form it takes helps ensure your mindset is in slow-thinking, reflective mode before acting or deciding. Repeating that interruption to nudge your mindset strengthens new neural pathways. We can get out of reacting to fear and see possibilities more quickly, even in new and unfamiliar situations. It's how we train our minds to see abundance, curiosity, and growth instead of fear.

## Designing Courage One Shift at a Time

Now that we've explored how fear influences actions, let's look at the second key component of this human-centered approach to change leadership: ***behavior design.***

You might not have considered that the smallest element of change is a single behavior, or that good change leadership comprises many small behaviors you consistently do. As author and scientist BJ Fogg documents in his behavior change model, when it comes to making new behaviors stick, the key is making it easy. That way, even when you're not motivated, you can still do it. High motivation levels at the onset trick our brains into thinking we can do hard things, which is why many people start but don't stick with a behavior change when motivation levels inevitably fall. There's a sweet spot with stretching to a place that's motivationally challenging for growth yet doesn't seem impossible.

When designing for behavior change, assuming low motivation makes the behavior more likely to last. High achievers struggle with this, as the desire to push to do more, better, and faster runs deep. As is often the case during change, a time crunch exacerbates this. The small shifts at the end of each chapter in this book are easy behaviors you can start doing immediately. The online mini-course and downloadable tool kit also helps you practice these behaviors after you understand the book's core concepts. Through repetition, your behavior will become more automatic; and a habit will form, allowing you to direct your attention elsewhere. That's when you can increase the difficulty level. When you try a new behavior several times and it's not sticking, this is a clue that you need to make it easier.

Because you're building the plane as it's flying during change, you may be feeling incredible pressure to "get it right" fast. Instead, make it easy and apply it quickly to the situation so that you can learn. Most adult learning happens on the job, which is excellent because applying what you know makes it more likely to stick. That's the upside. But you'll need to notice when you've reached your capacity and throttle down the airspeed.

This same thinking applies to your team. Individuals, teams, and organizations eventually reach the threshold for what they can and are motivated to do. Many teams and organizations are already experiencing change overload, with low motivation and capacity to learn more. Change asks you and your team to keep bumping that upper limit, which feels chronically uncomfortable. You set the pace by gauging your team's responses to determine when it's too many behaviors to change at once—and, therefore, when you need to slow down or make things easier.

As you review the behaviors throughout this book to improve your change leadership, ask yourself, "Do I already do this behavior consistently?"

If your answer is yes, proceed by adding another new behavior. Generally, you want to limit the number of new behaviors you add at any given time to no more than three. Once you do it successfully several times, proceed to the next one. Eventually, these become automatic habits, so you won't have to remember them consciously.

Fogg also shares the importance of celebrating anytime you perform a new behavior. It helps you feel good, which makes you want to do it again, as we all want to feel more pleasant emotions. There's an entire chapter in this book that's dedicated to rewarding behaviors to make them last for you and your team (see chapter 9).

## Cera Day's Story

Cera Day diligently reviews her email inbox to prioritize what she needs to do first. The volume of messages was high before, but now she can't keep up with all the project emails shared with her in addition to her day job. She catches herself by noticing how her body has tensed up. Her shoulders and neck are tight. She's clenching her jaw. She's still determining what came first: the apprehension about her workload, or the physical sensations.

It doesn't matter. She noticed the fear.

*What am I thinking right now?* Cera wonders. Taking a pause is new for her. Honestly, she's still determining whether it's necessary or just taking time away from doing the work. She's willing to try it, though, as her stress load has increased exponentially since the project started.

In that tiny moment of pausing, Cera notices that her approach to her email is compulsive. She wants to get everything done to feel a sense of control.

*I'm reacting*, she realizes. *I don't have enough time to get it all done.*

She laughs to herself, because there's truth in not having enough time. But she can't change that. She can choose how she wants to use her time. She knows she can continue reacting to the emails or try something else.

Cera closes out of her inbox and reflects on her most important priorities. That's enough to make her laugh at the absurdity of trying to keep up with the inflow of messages. She's unsure about what matters most for the project, but she knows where to find it.

She closes her laptop and walks out of her office to see who's here this early in the morning. A few conversations with her team members will be more fruitful than playing Whac-A-Mole with her never-ending email inbox. The intel can help Cera return to her inbox with a broader lens on her priorities, including what will help her people most.

She already feels more in control and energized.

## *One Small Shift:*
## NUDGING YOUR RESPONSE

As a leader during a significant organizational change, you are on a bullet train to personal growth. Kudos for taking the first step in maximizing this learning opportunity! It is a marathon, and the way to finish it with a smile is by focusing on one mile—and one step—at a time.

As you start, find comfort in knowing your fear is part of being human. Noticing body sensations to recognize fear's presence is an underutilized asset. It'll help you at work during change, and it may help your overall health. Nudging your mindset when you notice fear is an easy behavior that lets you stop reacting and start responding. Slowing down your response matters to your team, which can motivate and remind you about why you want to change what you are doing when you feel fear. The more you practice this one small shift, the easier it gets for your brain.

You are becoming the courageous leader your team needs, one small behavior shift at a time. Who knows where it may lead? You may even learn to let fear inspire you because it tells you something big is just around the corner. Now the fun begins!

# Putting It Into Practice
*free mini-course and downloadable tool kit*

Reading this book will provide you with an understanding of core concepts, models, and techniques to lead organizational change. To help you put these ideas into practice, access the free mini-course that includes downloadable tools. Find more support here:

https://www.krisjennings.com/Inspiredtoolkit

# Heroes Find Masters to Learn From

# 2

# WHAT IF I FAIL?

*Choosing the Hero's Journey*

It's been several months since the big project kickoff. Cera Day has assembled a team with a consulting partner and a dedicated internal project manager, Sergio, to implement the technology. Several of her team members hold part-time roles on the project (in addition to their day jobs). Doing double duty will help them gradually transition into their responsibilities in the "new" world, even if it means burning the candle at both ends for the short term.

One of her team members, Maria, arrives at Cera's office a few minutes early for her biweekly one-to-one meeting. With wide eyes and frenetic movement, Maria pulls out the desk chair and abruptly sits down before Cera can look up from her laptop. Maria does not currently have responsibilities on the project team, so her furrowed brow and severe expression surprise Cera.

So does Maria's opening question: "Am I going to lose my job?" She continues anxiously with several more questions

## What If I Fail?

before Cera can respond. "Are there going to be layoffs after this project is done? If I'm not on the project, does that signal anything about my future here?"

Cera pushes back from her desk, folding her arms. The questions frustrate her, and she doesn't have time for what feels like handholding.

"Maria, I can't promise anything," she replies brusquely. "You know that." She knows the business case includes head count reductions, which they hope to accomplish through natural attrition. So she redirects the questions to other catch-up topics and cuts the meeting short. Maria's slumped shoulders tell Cera she didn't handle the conversation well.

Before returning to her email and heading to the next meeting, Cera starts thinking about her own job. *What will happen to me if the project doesn't go well?*

The fear hits her hard. Her shoulders tense, and her mouth feels dry. *What if I fail?* She feels the bullseye set squarely on her. Her mind quickly spirals to other thoughts:

*Why was I, not one of my peers, asked to lead this project?*

*Are they planning to eliminate me if I don't lead the team well?*

*Do they know that what I'm being asked to do is impossible?*

*They're setting me up. I don't have to take this. I can leave.*

Cera doesn't notice her body's physical responses; her active mind fixates on the anxious questions. She clenches her desk and grits her teeth. The adrenaline prepares her for a fight. She made many sacrifices as a manager and has fought to get to where she is now.

She didn't have a choice about leading this project. Yet now that she's in it, she sees the near impossibility of achieving success. She'll have to work extraordinary hours and get her team to do the same. It's not fair, and that makes her angry. Even team members like Maria, who aren't on the project, add to her stress levels. It's all too much.

Cera runs through her options. What about leaving the company? The job market's hot right now, and she regularly gets calls from headhunters for similar roles in other organizations. She could find one like the "old" organization and return to how it was. That would be easy. She's confident she could run a team like that again.

Or, she could wiggle her way out of this situation by using the upcoming busy season as an excuse to hand off the project to a peer. It wouldn't be unthinkable to make that happen. She could also delegate to her team and put more visibility on them while taking the spotlight off herself.

Cera doesn't know what she will do about this anxious feeling, but she knows one thing for sure: Failure is not an option.

## Becoming the Hero

When everything happens fast and time feels crunched, we skip over things we think might slow us down. Our reactions to a stressful event often occur so quickly and automatically that we fail to notice the connections between our minds, bodies, and actions (see Figure 1 on the following page):

As we've already learned, our minds take shortcuts during stress to help us solve problems quickly based on predictions. We jump to an answer based on pattern recognition from

## Slowing Down Fear Reactions

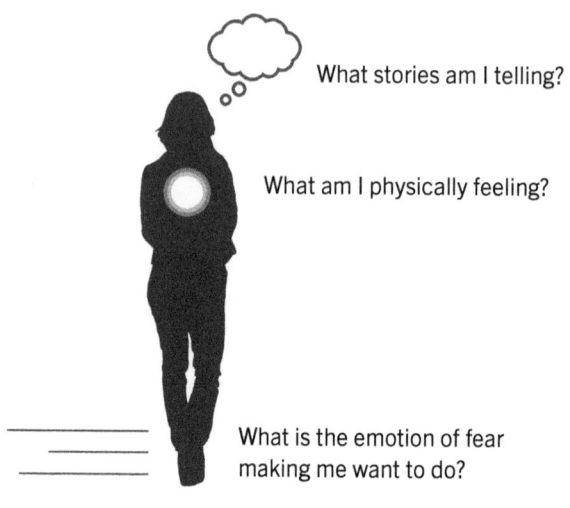

*Figure 1*

previous experiences. Under duress, we tend to automatically act out specific roles based on the beliefs or stories we've told ourselves that explain or justify our predictions. If you are someone who was repeatedly told and encouraged to solve your problems independently, and over time you learned you could do that effectively, you may already have a hero's mindset. On the other hand, if you learned to wait for others to help or weren't as effective at resolving issues, you may have a more passive mindset. You might have been told or learned that these situations were someone else's fault. In this mindset, you behave as a victim to a villain in the story.

The three roles of victim, villain, and hero are present in the hero's journey story archetype, one of the most recognized story patterns. It follows this flow: The hero represents an "average" person with an OK life and sets out on an adventure, searching for something better. Along the way, they experience setbacks (often in the form of a "bad" actor doing something malevolent to the innocent hero). The villain creates a victim out of the beloved hero—but only for as long as it takes the hero to defeat the villain, overcome the situation, and ultimately find "something better" triumphantly. The Star Wars series is an excellent example of the hero's journey story pattern.

How people experience change follows a pattern like the hero's journey. Figuratively speaking, you're journeying from where you are (i.e., it's "good") through trials and tests (i.e., the "bad," or typically difficult part during the middle) to find "something better." The plot has just thickened because you, the leader, realize how "bad" the complex parts will be for you and your team. You will become the hero by choosing that mindset and continuing to solve challenges to help your team throughout the journey instead of playing the game of "victim versus villain." Your example helps your team activate their own hero's journey to follow your lead courageously, even when things get scary and uncertain.

Stepping into the unknown frightens you, though, and you want to avoid feeling that way. This may result in you taking on the victim mindset. You may begin blaming others for putting you in this position. You may even feel like the change is being forced upon you. When you catch yourself using "me versus them" wording in an oppositional manner—which signals a victim mindset—it's time to remember what the hero would do. A victim stays in fear of the villain, while a hero acts despite it.

It's a quick step from feeling fear to telling a story about it, such as making your organization (or even a specific person) the villain. You can rewrite your story and interpret it another way by stepping into the hero role above the drama triangle, as authors Jim Dethmer, Diana Chapman, and Kaley Warner Klemp call it in their book, *The 15 Commitments of Conscious Leadership*. A hero takes responsibility for their thoughts, feelings, and actions; and encourages others to do the same. The hero uses the situation as an opportunity for expansion and adventure. They know they will face challenges, but they head out on the journey anyway because it's the right thing to do and serves a noble purpose: helping others.

## Identifying Advisers for Your Adventure

In most hero stories, the hero meets other characters and brings them along on the journey. Each character provides guidance, expertise, and help in some way. Plus, the camaraderie and personalities make the journey more fun! It's part of the experience; we love cheering for the hero and their expanded supporting cast.

On the other hand, leaders sometimes think that asking for help signals weakness or wastes precious resources. This represents another outdated mindset. Navigating an unfamiliar situation and making wise decisions quickly requires guidance from more experienced people. (Even Obi-Wan Kenobi calls in other Jedi for help.) It also affirms staying in the role of hero on a quest.

By creating an informal advisory council, you surround yourself with experts in the areas where you most need help. It's OK to ask for what you need in these relationships; most support should flow toward you. This can happen at whatever frequency best supports you. You may reach out frequently to some advisers and rarely to others.

Your advisory council may include:

- **A colleague willing to listen to you about challenges and brainstorm potential actions that can help you bring more neutrality to your decisions.** Someone with high empathy can support you during the hardest "bad" parts, even if they're not a subject matter expert.
- **Outside licensed help professionals**, such as a licensed therapist or personal coach, to help you recognize your emotions, thoughts, and behavior patterns.
- **Outside business professionals**, such as program advisers, change consultants, or leadership coaches, to provide you with independent guidance to navigate the path in general and on specific strategic or sensitive decisions. Outside perspectives help you see past the internal resistance of "we've always done it that way."
- **Coaching programs with other leaders,** which may include "hot seat" coaching so you can bring up a particular topic and receive feedback from other executives.
- **Dedicated checkpoints with your boss** to discuss your personal growth, not just status updates. Asking for time focused on your needs will allow you to clarify your success criteria. You can also ask for recommendations and introductions to other informal advisers within the organization.
- **Peers in other organizations** who have implemented similar changes.

- **A business change lead from your team** who can serve as your chief lieutenant in managing the change activities, along with your project manager. (More on this role is coming in chapter 4.)

Your advisory council consists of people who stand up to help you. You probably already know who these people are; you just need to ask for their support. These individuals can give you another perspective on your fears, and some of them will have done it before. That deepens your insight into what's coming, which should alleviate uncertainty. Start the process with each of your advisers by formally requesting support, stating what type of support you need, and doing your best to forecast the frequency. Set the expectation that your requests will often come ad hoc and that you intend the support to last for the duration of your change. Essentially, you're setting limits around what you need from your advisers to reassure them of their time commitment and clarify what type of guidance you want. With paid professionals, you'll also scope out a specific engagement plan, of course.

## Hearing How the Story Ends

Obi-Wan helps Luke Skywalker navigate his journey because Obi-Wan has traveled it before and has an even broader network to call upon to guide the young hero. Building a network with peers in other organizations who recently completed a similar change helps you anticipate what's coming. And more importantly, it guides your team to hear how the story ends.

Gathering outside input at the start of a change helps you build a more targeted project plan, including change activities, based on what you learn. It allows you to hear how other organizations handled specific decisions or issues and how their choices played out now that it's months or years later. The ideal peer benchmark will be similar in size, industry, complexity, type of workforce, and the amount of change the project introduced. This can require delicate maneuvers, as some organizations reject outside perspectives and respond with comments such as, "We don't do it that way here." But that's precisely when it's needed most to reduce insular thinking.

Change serves as a fantastic moment to bring outside perspectives into your organization. Doing this as a collective leadership team exercise helps the group come to a clear consensus while crystalizing concrete ways of what "something better" looks and feels like. It also balances out the horror stories your team has undoubtedly heard through the grapevine or dreamed up about the "bad" part of the journey. Facilitating a way for them to discover what's possible activates learning and, in a way, makes them part of the crew traveling together on the journey. During exercises such as this, while you may involve a broader team, you act as the facilitator of the process because you're in the best position to shape the narrative with the additional information you possess.

This type of learning happens through a variety of forums. During the information gathering, stay focused on learning what "something better" looks and feels like. Choose the forums that work best for you and your organization, including (but not limited to):

- Top-to-top conversations with leaders in other organizations, where you pair yourself with individuals in other organizations with the same job title

- Select members of your team with their peers in other organizations
- Industry conferences that you or select team members attend
- Online community forums

The key moment of creating wisdom out of this exercise is to ask your team to discuss it with one another by sharing what they learned. During the early days of a change, dedicate time away from the daily routine to discuss how the team envisions "something better." Asking the team questions that evoke pleasant emotions can help you cultivate the hopeful outlook that defeating the (hypothetical) evil empire on this hero's journey may be possible because others have done it, too.

## Working Toward "Something Better"

Regardless of the organization, department, industry, or technology, projects maintain this universal set of success standards:

- Whether the project went live on time (i.e., time)
- Whether the project came in on or under budget (i.e., cost)
- Whether the project delivered the requirements identified (i.e., quality)

However, you can deliver on all three project constraints and still fail on the people side. If the people impacted by the change are stuck back in "good" or never progress past "bad," the vision of "something better" will fail to come alive. It will also fail to come to fruition if you don't have a plan for getting there or adequately describe it in an emotionally compelling way that inspires and encourages behavior change.

Part of your role is educating others on what ***people success*** looks like and then managing the team members assigned to the tasks that represent mile markers on the journey. This is the tangible story of "something better." People want to know there's a plan to help you out of the "bad" part. Your project manager will take the lead on documenting change activities, including visibly reporting progress in team meetings and tracking the completion of the ***project plan***. While your organization may use a specific methodology for delivering projects (Agile and Waterfall are the two most common methods) or even use a standard change management methodology, it's important for you to understand fundamental change activities so you can ensure they're completed in your project and documented in your project plan milestones:

- Identifying roles within business processes
- Performing gap analyses to document differences between current knowledge and skills and what's needed in the future
- Ensuring individuals understand their role(s) and responsibilities
- Documenting behaviors to measure adoption
- Creating a rewards plan to encourage adoption
- Transition support activities (stakeholder engagement, communications, testing, and training are common activities)

You and your business change lead will influence shifts in behaviors through relationships and ongoing conversations with individuals and groups. These activities are ad hoc and not captured in the project plan, but they are vitally important to influencing your change's success. (More on these activities is coming in chapter 6.)

## Setting Expectations for Reaching "Something Better"

Sometimes leadership expects change to look like the Death Star exploding—a giant, visible moment of success in the mission. It blows up, everyone has a party, and then they move on. The change is done. But it doesn't usually work that way. Most of the time, change is not a big-bang event, over and done in one day. Day one is often quiet, with much effort to support adoption yet to come.

Author and organizational consultant William Bridges differentiates ***change*** from ***transition*** in this way. Change, like the project going live, can be represented as a date on a calendar. Transition describes the broader migration to new beliefs and behaviors. People success means supporting your team until they fully adopt new behaviors, which happens after they've had time to practice new skills and apply new knowledge. So, behavioral consistency—or people success—typically occurs months after a specific change date.

If your boss doesn't yet understand this difference, educating them accordingly will help you create specific and realistic success measures for you as a change leader. Using the tasks identified in partnership with your project manager, prepare for a conversation with your boss (and other leadership stakeholders

## Choosing the Hero's Journey

as needed) to develop a shared understanding of people success and the timeline for completing the transition. You may also want to include in this conversation the other support requests you identified during your advisory council exercise, such as asking for dedicated coaches, program advisers, group coaching, a business change lead, or change professionals.

Here's what this managing-up conversation with your boss may look like:

> **YOU:** "I'd like to request some input about your expectations. What does success in this change look like to you?"
>
> **YOUR BOSS:** "Most importantly, this has got to be delivered on time and within budget. I can't have the business blaming me for not delivering it when we promised."
>
> **YOU:** "Those are absolutely criteria for the project and the technology aspects. Our project manager's support gives us great visibility into both factors. It's easy to know whether we meet them, too. But what about the people side? What does that look like in terms of success?"
>
> **YOUR BOSS:** "Well, we need to train people. And I want people to be excited about it. We've waited a long time for this, and it's a big investment for the organization."
>
> **YOU:** "I understand where you're coming from. Ideally, I want people to be excited, too. Addressing emotions is an important part of the change; I

already notice some fear that may turn into resistance. So I want to ask a pointed follow-up question: Is it good enough to deliver training? Or do we need to do more? To ensure people can do what they need for their roles?"

**YOUR BOSS:** "When you say 'make sure,' that sounds like we're going to hand-hold. I don't want it to drag out or take too much time. It's not solely our responsibility; people must own that for themselves, too. It must be as easy as possible and take as little time as possible. If we take the business out of production to train them, it's got to be effective at getting them to do what they need to do—and fast. No downtime because of the change."

**YOU:** "I hear what you're saying. Those are ambitious goals when it comes to our training. When do you expect change activities to be completed?"

**YOUR BOSS:** "By the launch date."

**YOU:** "OK. I want to clarify that expectation. It won't be possible for us to deliver training before things are fully ready, which is the launch date. We plan on training business users immediately after the launch, but it'll take time for them to get good at it. **We need more people support in the few months after going live.** There will be a period when work will take longer. If that's what you mean by 'no downtime,' then we need to discuss what's realistic."

*Choosing the Hero's Journey*

**YOUR BOSS:** "That makes sense, and I know you're right. But we'll need to manage those expectations with key leaders—including the steering committee—so they're not surprised. Are you prepared to discuss training and timing with them?"

**YOU:** "Yes. Does that look like one-to-one conversations? Or discussions at our next steering committee meeting?"

**YOUR BOSS:** "Both. A few steering committee members will need a preview before the group meets."

**YOU:** "Great. **I want to start managing expectations around people success early.** They will see our progress on the project plan. Here's a copy of those key activities and the timing for completing them." (This is when you can share a print copy of the critical change activities from the project plan, including due dates.)

**YOUR BOSS:** "Thanks. This helps me understand the process and see how you will track progress against it. What support do you need from me?"

**YOU:** "Thank you for asking. I need help in a few areas: managing the role analysis, and developing the communications and training materials. These aren't skills our current team has, nor does our project manager have the capacity to support them. I am dedicating a team member to overseeing the coordination through a business change lead role. But that individual will need help from experts. I want to gather some estimates to analyze costs."

## What If I Fail?

**YOUR BOSS:** "Great. Let's revisit this when you've gathered the numbers. I can see that you're taking this change seriously, which we haven't done well as an organization. The more tangible we can make what we're doing clear and the more transparently we share that with my peers, the more credibility we'll build for what we're doing."

An alignment conversation like this one with your boss ensures consistent expectations around people success and how you plan on achieving it through change activities. Often, this looks and feels quite different from past change because it is more tangible and measurable. When you define success clearly, you remove failure from the picture.

## Cera Day's Story

Cera Day beams with excitement. She's giddy with ideas about how to support her people. She's just returned from a conversation with a peer in another organization who shared how their project transformed their team's work. That team is now working more strategically. What was fuzzy about the transition became clearer, including a realistic timetable for getting there. She feels less uncertain about what it will take and how to succeed on the people side. She hasn't felt this hopeful in months.

Cera has heard that getting to "something better" will take persistent effort, but she knows more about what to expect and what she can do. She feels reaffirmed in her decision to add specific support to the team and organize her own informal advisory council of experts. It's giving her places to ask questions and remove doubt.

## Choosing the Hero's Journey

Cera has also identified a team member, Athena, as her business change lead. Together with Sergio, Cera's project manager, they added key change activities to the master project plan to make sure everyone has visibility to the work associated with supporting people success and how the work they do as a team contributes to it. As a team, they're starting to work together holistically to tackle all elements of success for the project—on time, on budget, on scope, and getting people ready. Cera has stopped playing small, as if she were a victim of the circumstances. She's now seeing the possibilities for her and her team. They're more certain about the future and feel more hopeful that it's doable with the plan they've built together.

When Cera presented the development role opportunity to Athena, Athena agreed to do it if she got help on some of the activities she'd never done before. They talked about adding help to complete role analysis and develop training materials. Athena believes she can handle other aspects, such as coordinating testing and communications. Cera now feels more confident about completing a comprehensive change plan and the resources assigned. They benchmarked ideas with other organizations who've done it before.

At the steering committee, Cera presented her plan for getting people ready, aligning expectations about the time investments for manager training and how long it'll take after going live to return to "normal" again. When other leaders started expressing the need to have everyone ready before the go-live date, Sophia jumped in with comments to clarify this.

It was a proud moment for Cera to watch her boss repeating the same language she'd used in their earlier, private discussion about training. It was sticking! Now Cera feels encouraged and less alone. She still feels doubt, apprehension, and uncertainty, but it's not keeping her from moving forward. When she has a question, she can quickly bounce it off someone within the cadre of people she's asked for help. Her head tilts slightly higher than it did before. A smile passes across her face, reflecting her hopefulness. Now that she possesses greater clarity of the project's success, failure doesn't seem imminent. She won't give up on herself or her team.

## *One Small Shift:*
## HEROES ASK FOR HELP

Uncertainty around expectations of people success with your boss and other key leaders contributes to feelings of self-doubt. It's easy for this to spiral into panic and self-protective mindsets and behaviors.

Shifting out of that state requires reframing your story—from the role of victim to the role of hero, and then gradually into the role of the wise elder, guiding the collective crew on the journey to "something better." You own your personal thoughts, feelings, and actions as a hero, including asking advisers for help, gathering intel on the story's ending, and building a plan to get through the "bad" part. Asking for help from experts and others who've done this before removes ambiguity around key success criteria that help you get in front of potential issues, such as setting expectations for the timeline to complete the transition.

Heroes know when to call upon others. Having courage means getting the help you need.

# You Cannot Control Everything, But You Can Influence a Lot

# 3

# IS ANYTHING IN MY CONTROL?

*Choosing to Influence Rather Than Micromanage*

As she does every Monday, Cera Day opens her calendar to view her schedule for the week ahead. She feels in control when she knows what's coming. She spots two meetings that require prep: her weekly status meeting with the implementation partner, and the monthly executive steering committee meeting. Cera's pulse quickens, and her jaw clenches. She briefly holds her breath without realizing it. She dreads the implementation meeting, as the topics can become detailed and tedious, but the steering meeting causes her anxiety. She's not used to interacting with a wide-ranging group of executives and business leaders looking to her for answers. *What might they throw at me this time?* she thinks.

On one hand, she recognizes that the group wants to help the project succeed. It also can feel like a game of Stump the Chump when random questions leave her tap-dancing. She's not good at hitting these curveballs; she keeps swinging and missing. Her shoulders tense, and her palms are even a bit sweaty as she considers how to prepare.

## Is Anything in My Control?

Lately, it feels nearly impossible for Cera to anticipate issues. The project has hit several speedbumps, creating rework. In one critical example, the team won't get everything they wanted incorporated into the technology. Should Cera preempt the questions from the steering committee by adding that topic to the agenda? She doubts herself and doesn't want to bring up what might look like a failure on her part. Sergio wanted to change the stoplight status from green to yellow to reflect this issue, but Cera insisted they stay on green. She doesn't want it to look like anything's not going well. She believes it'll reflect poorly on her leadership.

The business and IT teams discussed this issue for weeks. The requirement didn't sound complicated to Cera, but it is. It took several discussions to understand how much it would cost and how long the technical team would need to build it. Now, whenever this topic comes up, Cera feels irritated and impatient, and she catches herself rolling her eyes.

At first, Cera held her ground on the issue, sticking to the promised scope. It wasn't her fault that IT missed estimating the customization, making her even angrier. She's taking the blame for something that others failed to do. Ultimately, both cost and timeline constraints mean this customization must wait. Sharing the news with her team and her boss, Sophia, wasn't easy, and now Cera's disappointed.

Letting others down by breaking her promises is unfamiliar territory. She's always been the manager whom people could trust to get things done—which is why she's in this position, leading this project. She's capable of organizing work but uncomfortable in a space where things are more gray than black-and-white. She's not sure of anything anymore.

Cera also feels exposed in front of the steering committee,

as she doesn't know its members well. She's far from the expert in this space. She lacks a solid reputation of competency to rely on with them. Her stomach churns as she desperately looks for a thirty-minute window on her calendar to prepare for the steering committee meeting.

Cera wishes this would be over so that things can return to normal. She's guessing—and with those guesses, she has more doubts about herself and whether she can ever be good at this role. She asks herself out loud, "Is anything in my control?"

## Recognizing Areas of Influence

If you have ever cared for a goldfish (or any other kind of fish), you know that when you bring it home from the pet store, you must carefully transition it from the plastic bag to the larger aquarium that now serves as its home. You must also do many things to prepare the fish for the transition, including conditioning the water to ensure it has the appropriate nutrients and holds a temperature consistent with its existing environment. Typically, when you place a fish in its new home, it swims around frantically in circles to determine its boundaries.

Change feels like leaving the familiar comfort of one environment for an unknown—and potentially threatening—new one. When you find yourself dropped into a bigger bowl, the first thing to help yourself acclimate is to explore the edges. What can you control in this new place? Early Stoic philosophers used a model for situations such as this to help manage uncertainty. This philosophy was intended to guide individuals toward a more peaceful life. The Circles of Influence Model asks you to consider what's in your control, what you can influence, and things outside of your control that you must learn to accept.

## Circles of Influence Model

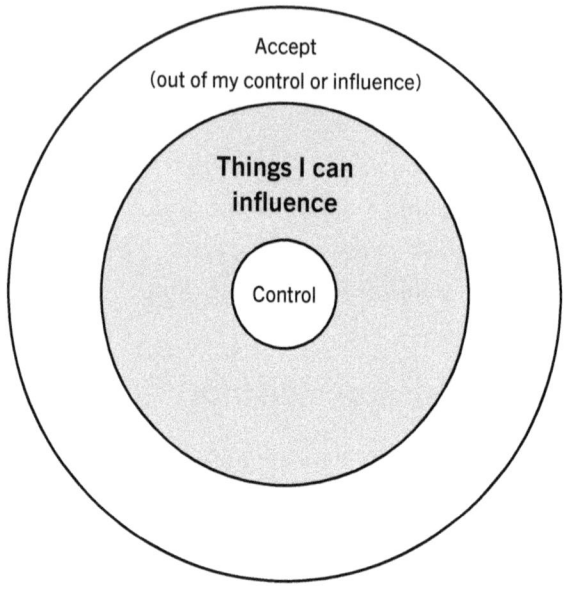

Figure 2

Starting with the model's outermost circle, there are many things outside of your control or influence in your role as a change leader. You cannot control the fact that humans, including you, have emotions. To fear unknown situations is human. But learning to accept rather than resist emotions—including fear—will bring you peace as a human being and a change leader. In the model's innermost circle, you can control your actions, including nudging yourself into a reflective response rather than automatically reacting when you notice the signals of fear in yourself. You can control stepping into the hero role, owning your thoughts, feelings, and actions. This turns something outside your control (fear) into something within it (how you respond to fear).

The middle circle is where the ambiguity lies in determining what you can influence. If you've succeeded in your career by controlling, you may overutilize this during times of change and think that the innermost circle is larger than it is. Many things that you think you can control, however, are areas you can influence. As a change leader, you can influence:

- Creating an environment that encourages change
- Treating change as a choice, not a command
- Rewarding choices immediately

Believing you can control change reflects a ***fixed mindset***, where possibilities are black or white and limited to binary outcomes of success or failure. During change, that leads to frustration because there are more gray areas. Rather than resisting the gray, embrace it as an opportunity to direct your influence and see various possibilities using a ***growth mindset***. Nudging yourself toward that mindset allows you to explore the new, bigger bowl more freely and with less fear about trying to control an outcome.

Let's dig deeper into where to direct your influence.

## Creating the Environment

One of the most important responsibilities of being a change leader is influencing your team's environment, also known as your organizational and team ***culture***. If the water you swim in has progressively become more polluted over time, it will make your goals more challenging to achieve. Change tends to make the water clarity levels in an environment evident quickly.

There are many aspects to a healthy culture, but ***psychological safety*** is one of the most important during change because of how it influences behaviors. In a culture that nurtures psychological safety, team members feel safe to express emotions and raise questions without fear of repercussions. Silence permeates an unsafe culture, where speaking up to ask a question risks looking uninformed—and may be penalized or reprimanded for not knowing the answer. Team members withhold information, ideas, and suggestions because they believe their contributions won't make a difference. And while less malicious in intent, some people don't speak up for lack of confidence, or they take a passive approach (which looks a lot like a victim mindset). Having something to say and feeling unable to say it is unpleasant. What's underneath that silence is a fear of not being valued.

That's quite the opposite of the ideal conditions for success during change. Your team has the best perspective on what works and what doesn't in their roles and processes. They have insights into the hidden barriers, including the perceptions from those outside the core team who aren't represented directly in the discussion room. Creating an environment where feelings, questions, and perspectives can be raised accelerates problem-solving. It gets in front of all the issues that *will* arise later. A psychologically safe environment encourages all types of conversations, including ideas that aren't well-formed or may need input from others to refine them. It also means sharing emotions constructively. As noted, feeling an emotion and having the words to discuss it don't come easily for everyone. But when they feel safe and valued, your team will find the courage to raise questions, issues, and emotions.

It takes consistent effort to create this type of environment. You nurture it through the behaviors you demonstrate, the structures you create, and the boundaries you set for nonadherence to your safety norms. It takes time to demonstrate behaviors consistently, but no matter the condition of your culture, you can improve it from where you are currently. Change can be used opportunistically to make dramatic shifts in your team culture. It's an ideal moment to throw away what's not serving collaborative innovation and start practicing new ways of operating. Some of those behaviors you demonstrate to influence the environment during change include transparency and vulnerability in your communications and listening more than you talk. We'll go much deeper into specific techniques you can use to influence in the moment to cultivate trust in your relationships during chapters 6 and 7.

In the meantime, you can gauge where you're at by asking a simple question during your one-to-one conversations with each team member: "Did you feel you could bring forward questions and concerns during our discussions of the change this week?" Listen responsively to the feedback you receive, and ask follow-up questions for clarification during each discussion. These private moments allow you to coach team members who need help phrasing a question or area of concern while inviting them into future discussions. When you consistently ask for this feedback, you demonstrate your sincere interest in improving. Doing this early on in a change makes your environment more conducive to success.

## Presenting Choices and Understanding Nudges

Change is a choice. When moving to a bigger bowl, you can stay in the known safety of the fish castle or dart out to explore the new environment. Dumping your team into the bigger bowl and demanding that they explore creates resistance because they inherently don't feel safe. That is not inviting participation to "opt in" to the change, but rather giving a forceful, threatening command.

Your team members have choices, the most basic of which is whether they want to stay on the team. Attracting and retaining the best talent means thinking about what you do through the lens of offering choices. Nudging your team toward a preferred choice is part of ongoing influencing in your leadership. During change, influencing is far more powerful than trying to command and control.

Choice activates ***intrinsic motivation***: "I choose to change because I believe it offers me benefits (tangible or intangible)." This type of motivation is stronger and lasts longer than extrinsic factors such as incentives or punishment. Choices, once made, are more likely to stick. This, too, is a mindset shift from attempting to control behaviors to one that uses free will to present options and influence others toward the preferred choice.

But let's face it: Influencing people to choose isn't easy. It's particularly challenging during change because people lack information, are unfamiliar with the options, and generally have too much going on in their heads to have the capacity to focus on the choice. They also don't want to feel the unpleasant emotions accompanying change, particularly fear. Oftentimes, they avoid making a choice because staying with the status quo is easier and less painful. When this happens, leaders sometimes find themselves in a power struggle to force the choice through the carrot and stick method. They offer financial incentives and force compliance, which creates underground resistance that shows up as an uninspired, uncommitted team who does what they're told.

Rather than forcing people to make big changes quickly, offer small choices to opt in gradually. This requires you to take on some of the thinking so that you can design small choices that move your team toward the end goal. While having options activates intrinsic motivation to choose, **nudges** encourage the preferred option. Behavioral economists Cass Sunstein and Richard Thaler developed their nudge theory out of the Nobel Prize-winning work of psychologists Daniel Kahneman and Amos Tversky. This theory recognizes that people behave irrationally, and often mistakenly. Nudges help people move in the desired direction. We can use this theory in change design by knowing that humans want to move away from unpleasant feelings and toward pleasant ones.

There are predictable ***peak experience moments*** during change when emotions are strongest: the lowest unpleasant ones, and the highest point of pleasant feelings. Using nudges, you influence others toward these peaks. You'll want to nudge toward getting through the low point of the hero's journey earlier in your timeline so that you can begin nudging toward "something better" and more pleasant emotions. Influencing behaviors using emotional nudges reduces the depth and duration of the low points and accelerates the pace toward reaching the high points. Chapter 6 will go into detail about how to design change for these peak experience moments using nudges.

## Rewarding Choices and Using Encouraging Language

A fast feedback loop that rewards choice helps change stick. When you offer a choice to opt in and a team member chooses it, reward it quickly. Immediately, a team member will feel good about making the choice, which makes them want to do more of it. When you offer choices to your entire team and some begin opting in, others will naturally want to make the same choice. Humans crave a feeling of belonging to the group and will choose to perform a behavior when they see it keeps their status within it. It's the role of the leader to notice choices to opt in and reward it visibly so that others follow.

One simple statement can help you immediately reward choices at any stage of a change: "I believe in you." Use it to cultivate a sense of belonging and approval from you, the group leader. You can say it in response to many challenging situations to influence others to opt in. (This is an example of an emotional nudge.) This encouragement from you will help ignite intrinsic motivation, like in these scenarios:

- "I hear how scared you are. You want to know what's coming and how we'll get there. I believe it's possible when we work together. We will figure it out together. I believe in you."

- "This change is challenging for all of us, including me. There have been times when I've been ready to throw in the towel. But then I remembered how it could be better for our team. I won't give up, and I believe in you, too."

- "The more I learn about what we're building and how it will help our team, the more excited I am about the possibilities. I can see how we will support managers more strategically. We'll have answers to questions quickly that take weeks to gather today. The climb is steep, but I believe in our team. And I believe in you."

Saying positive, encouraging statements to your team throughout change is one of the easiest and most powerful ways to influence behavior change. It tells your team you notice their effort, which makes a huge difference in them wanting to keep trying. Say it to yourself, too: "I believe in you."

## Cera Day's Story

The steering committee members remain quiet as Sergio, the project manager, shares an update on the timeline and budget. Cera Day also stays silent, as this isn't her moment to shine. Her eyes and attention remain on Sergio to indicate her engagement and confidence that he can handle this.

When it comes time to provide a people update, Cera changes the dynamic in the meeting by asking the committee, "How are you feeling about our progress?" She notices some awkward shuffles, and several committee members avoid eye contact with her. They're not used to contributing to these meetings. They're also not sure if it's safe to share their feelings. This group is familiar with other members but has never come together to oversee a significant work effort. Cera recognizes that the group must feel psychologically safe to maximize the value of their input, including their willingness to influence their leadership peers throughout the organization. Allowing them to stand on the sidelines isn't going to build the collaborative problem-solving this change needs from them.

To get the feedback flowing, Cera asks a more pointed question to one of the business leaders with whom she'd started regular input check-ins several weeks ago: "How could this improve the information flow between managers and HR?" She knows that putting this business leader on the spot is risky, but it is a calculated choice to nudge participation.

Cera remains calm and poised, and her body language shows she is receptive to listening. Standing in front of this group intimidated her just a few months ago. She was in unfamiliar territory with executives who didn't know her strengths. At first, Cera worried that this group of leaders, not knowing her managerial prowess, was a liability for her. She wanted to control what they thought about her by limiting what she said or did to only when she was 100 percent certain of an answer. Now, she's letting go of that need to micromanage and focusing on how she can influence their actions to support the change. Establishing her reputation in their minds as an **influential leader** is much easier because they don't have fixed perceptions.

After each comment, Cera makes sure to affirm the other executives quickly. She uses "I believe" language to connect each idea to feeling optimistic about the future. She catches herself when she wants to react to an uninformed opinion, as she's most focused on creating an environment where all ideas are welcome. She accepts that others still fear the unknown of the change, making a note to follow up with a private discussion where she can influence by nudging. Cera sees the group as curious about this discussion, which gives her hope about their capability to have richer dialogues during future meetings as they develop more psychological safety to share. She can't control all the variables of this change, but ironically she feels more in control now that she knows where to spend her time and energy influencing.

*One Small Shift:*
## INFLUENCING CHOICES

Becoming an influential change leader doesn't happen overnight. New behaviors start and get practiced over time. When you consistently show up to ask for feedback, listen, and encourage others, you gradually increase psychological safety and reduce fear. Getting people to talk and share without fear of repercussion is a preceding step to getting them to behave differently. Giving them a choice to change helps them want to opt in. Any fear they feel will be immediately reduced by you noticing and encouraging the choice, and they'll want to do more of the new behavior.

Shifting out of tendencies to control is a gradual process. Leading change allows you to practice that evolution and let others see you in a new, more influential light.

People Influence People

# 4

# WHY ARE WE DOING THIS?

*Developing Your People*

Cera Day notices Caral is unusually quiet during today's department team meeting. Her eyes glaze over, and her focus drifts as Sergio, the project manager, reviews timeline details. The neat boxes and colorful lines of the Gantt chart should help the team feel more certain about the work, but Cera doubts that the details are having that effect.

Cera knows that Caral is hardworking. *What's bothering her today?* Cera wonders. Caral watches Sergio click through the presentation slides while listening to him explain the details of this week's tasks, but it doesn't appear she understands what he's saying. Her eyes watch the screen, but they're not focused and sharp.

Cera takes in the rest of the team, sitting around the small conference room table. Adir is discretely playing on his phone; and Maria is feverishly taking notes, although Cera can't be sure she's writing about what's happening in the meeting room, as her head is focused only on the paper in front of her. Manuel is leaning back in his chair, watching the clock, and sipping his coffee. Sergio meticulously reviews details of the work that needs to get done, but Cera suspects the team isn't internalizing what those details mean.

Sergio pauses and asks, "Any questions?"

Radio silence. Not a single question from the team.

In the past decade, Cera has learned the ins and outs of her team members' strengths and styles. They all handle stress in different ways, and it shows up most often during their busiest period at the end of the year. However, since most have been in their roles for several years, even that stress response is predictable and manageable. For the most part, they handle challenges with ease. They're comfortable.

Feeling comfortable is dangerous. It hasn't helped the team prepare for this project; the body language and lack of engagement around the table today tell Cera that her team isn't actively preparing. They're sitting back, waiting. They aren't clear about what's expected of them or confident they can do it. They don't even know what questions to ask to clarify things for themselves. Fear responses—fight, flight, freeze, and fawn—are present in her team.

Cera's starting to realize the depth of her team's doubt. They're not sure what is involved in this significant effort everyone's talking about. Is it more than just a new technology system? How will their day-to-day work change? It's so big and ambitious that none of the team members have a good idea of the overall picture, let alone their roles. They are afraid they don't know where to start clarifying by asking Sergio questions.

The timeline and activity details don't help them understand how their worlds change, which means they're not sure where to start digging in to learn. In their fear, they're dutifully waiting to be told precisely what to do. Cera reinforced that behavior over the years through her command-and-control management style. Now that she needs them to independently explore what this means for them, she recognizes the gap in her leadership behaviors. They're waiting for someone to give them explicit instructions so they can dutifully do them.

Cera can almost read the minds of her team around this table, even if they aren't speaking the words out loud:

- **Caral:** "When we put in System Y, it took months for things to return to normal. They promised it would make our work easier, but it didn't. I just kept using my paper tracking. It was easier than the system. Most people who worked on that project aren't even here anymore."
- **Adir:** "I'll wait until someone tells me what to do. I've got enough on my plate, and I don't need to worry about something that might not even happen."
- **Manuel:** "I'm less than five years from retirement. I've just got to ride this thing out like all the other projects that have come and gone. Corporate gets these ideas, but they don't last. Poor Cera. She will go down with the ship, just like the others."
- **Maria:** "What are they trying to tell us? I'm lost. I'll ask Cera privately later what I'm supposed to do."

Cera feels confident about the factors within her control, like the budget and timeline. But as she looks at each of her team members, she knows that's not truly what will make the project successful. She will have failed if her team doesn't use the new system and its powerful analytics. Without making that leap, they won't survive in the new world. She sees it coming, even if the team doesn't understand that yet. Their fear is holding them back. She's now fighting her fear-based reaction of controlling them by issuing directive orders for them to follow.

Cera feels protective of her team. She wants them to succeed, but she doubts all of them will. Some need a massive skills upgrade to think differently about their work; others will struggle with the technology. Taking steps toward that future will be difficult. They've been comfortable for so long that this new way feels intimidating, even if she's promising it will be "better."

None of them believe it's possible. They doubt themselves, the organization's commitment, and her. She wants to influence them forward but isn't sure how when there's so much doubt.

Cera looks around the conference room to meet each of their gazes momentarily. Sergio's been waiting patiently for her to speak up.

The question on her mind and everyone else's is, "Why are we doing this?"

## Leading People versus Managing Tasks

Why are you making this change? There are undoubtedly specific business reasons. You've probably answered that question from your boss and leadership team peers dozens of times. Those reasons may be that it closes a market competitiveness gap, helps your business grow, automates processes, or creates operational efficiency.

Many logical and strategic reasons exist for why. Yet the answer underneath the business rationale is simple: to improve team performance. Humans make change happen. Leading change is about helping people grow. It's bridging a gap between where they are and where they need (and want) to be.

But all the extra work that accompanies change feels like being stuck in quicksand that keeps pulling you in deeper. It's daunting to look at what's on your to-do list, and your fear of getting all the tasks done might distract you from the more important responsibility of developing the people who will enable the change vision. After all, behind the task lists are "your" humans: the team of people you hired over the years and whom you've worked alongside. You have relationships with these people, and these relationships are critical to the strategic goal of getting from here to there.

The real reason why for change is developing your people. By keeping people development top of mind and on top of your to-do list, you tap into a powerful source of altruistic motivation about service to others. When you're anxious and apprehensive about getting everything done, this understanding can help you prioritize your limited time toward what matters most: people.

Let's explore what it means to put people first during change by examining how the Human-Centered Change Model operationalizes this philosophy (see Figure 3 on the following page). The model has two axes: time orientation (short- or long-term), and attention (tasks or people).

Most organizations focus exclusively on the model's left side through a task orientation. They define all the things that need to get done and organize them into a manageable list (also known as a project plan). This is a natural place to start. It addresses short-term needs in definable activities of informing through communications and training on "how to." It's easier

Why Are We Doing This?

### Human-Centered Change Model

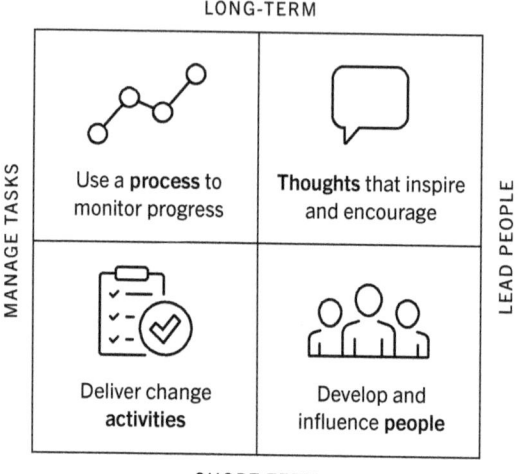

*Figure 3*

to control tasks; and as organizations need to implement more change faster (especially those driven by technology), many put a repeatable process in place. This meets both short- and longer-term objectives. This left side of the model is what most people think of today when they hear the phrase "change management."

So why do most changes still fail?

There's more to change than tasks. The other half of the model focuses on the human element of leading people. This is **change leadership** that inspires, encourages, develops, and influences people. The right side of the model is the why of change. A human-centered approach to change focuses on people and the relational aspect of how people influence people. Through relationships, leaders inspire and encourage people toward something new. Relationships and a sense of belonging to the group are the magnet that pulls people forward even when that something is uncertain and ambiguous. It helps people act even while they're scared.

So, why are you doing this? Your people. How will you get them from here to there? Your words and actions start in the upper right quadrant of the model with a long-term focus and attention on people. This quadrant is yours to own. If it feels scary right now because you don't know what it looks like or how to do it, it'll become less intimidating through the remaining chapters that will help you learn how to inspire, encourage, develop, and influence people during change.

All quadrants of the Human-Centered Change Model support change adoption. When you use all four quadrants, you are more likely to accelerate behavior shifts and reach higher levels of team performance. But that doesn't mean you do everything. Not doing everything allows you the time and capacity to focus on the areas that can only come from you, namely the long-term people efforts.

To fully leverage the model, you'll need to engage and develop two other key roles: your project manager, and your business change lead. The three of you will work together to implement the change.

A **business change lead** is a unique and temporary development role within this model. It is sourced from within your team and serves an essential purpose in influencing because it leverages existing relationships. This individual helps you influence others, primarily through conversations with their peers on your team. This person becomes a key ally for you and a place to begin building momentum. If you can do it with one person, you can have a ripple effect on behavior change, knowing that people influence people.

## Answering the Question of *Why*

Let's explore each quadrant of the Human-Centered Change Model more fully, starting with the upper right, which is singularly your responsibility: to inspire and encourage others through thought delivery. This is you consistently and frequently conveying a compelling *why* for your change. It starts early and continues with proof point updates throughout your change to provide evidence of progress. The task accomplishments you achieve on the model's left side show that the change is doable, which encourages your team to keep going. However, the tasks are just tasks unless you help make a specific connection with how they support the vision of helping your people grow. This turns the *why* into a more compelling emotional version of the story.

The difference in the model is that you share those examples. It's not something to ask your project manager or another team member to do. You have the most power to influence your team during change. Your progress updates that celebrate accomplishments and recognize contributions toward the vision are simple, cost-effective ways to encourage change (more about rewarding change in chapter 9). Your team listens to what you say about the *why* and pays attention to whether you notice their efforts. Immediate and frequent feedback from you is a key behavior within this model. It's not something that you can delegate to a project manager or subordinate without sacrificing impact. When these leadership behaviors are absent, change becomes just another set of extra tasks and activities that need to get done. The change gets "managed," but without change leadership, it fails to develop and influence people to achieve a higher level of performance and engagement.

If the big *why* for any change is about developing people, your role is critical to successfully implementing it. You serve as the pivot point between the vision and the execution. Fundamental aspects of enabling your vision include knowing who needs to do what and how that's different from today. To strategically manage the transition, you'll monitor progress by observing the behaviors of your people. If you do this well, you will literally know it when you see it along the way and have a good idea of whether you're on track.

Observing behaviors directly correlates to your encouraging actions. You observe, recognize, or correct, and then move on to the next behavior. You encourage and influence behavior shifts in your team in an iterative manner through the regular interactions you have with them. You want to help them get better, and they want to learn because of that human connection with you. A **behavior-based road map** helps you understand the timeline for these shifts and gives you specific things to watch for in your team. You see progress along the way.

## Managing the Process (Your Project Manager)

As you work with your project manager and your business change lead to implement the change, together you will create a core change team that both manages tasks and leads people. The three of you will also influence many other people known as **stakeholders**. These individuals include:

- **Project team members** with specific assignments as tracked on the project plan (e.g., workstream leads for specific functional areas, a dedicated testing lead)

- **Subject matter experts** who contribute occasionally (e.g., technical or functional advisers who inform the design)
- **Interested parties who are not directly involved** on the project team but have a vested interest in the result (e.g., the members of your team who will use the solution)
- **Executives** who approve financial funding
- **End users** in your organization (e.g., leaders who will use the reports, managers and employees who will use the system)

In a complex project, another set of people is involved through the external partners hired to implement the solution. These may include:

- **A consulting executive partner/adviser** who ensures you, the client, are satisfied with how the work progresses
- **A program or project manager** who organizes the project activities and ensures work is completed satisfactorily by the consulting team members
- **Consulting workstream leads** who are responsible for a specific functional area and who partner with your project workstream leads to ensure functional requirements are met
- **Consulting subject matter experts** with narrow advisory roles, which may include technical solution architecture, security, and potential support for

change activities, such as communications or training materials development

Whew! How do you keep track of all these people and their work *and* keep them informed and engaged? By having a well-coordinated core change team—you, your project manager, and your business change lead—with clear responsibilities for the tasks and relationships among your key stakeholders.

Your project manager organizes the process and tasks on the model's left side. They manage scope, budget, and deadlines. This helps deliver the project on time and within budget while satisfying quality requirements. Your project manager also enables you to determine how to represent people activities on key project artifacts, such as the project plan, the RAID (Risks, Assumptions, Issues, and Decisions) log, and the project timeline. They help you measure progress on people activities and overall success criteria (aka the upper left quadrant of the model).

Yet, as your project manager primarily manages the tasks, they also see and hear invaluable data about people's behavior. They're gathering this through the team meetings, the activities tracked on the project plan, and (more anecdotally) the comments shared about the work. This role is crucial to your people success because the project manager sees behaviors and hears feedback that you don't. Your project manager helps you adjust your change leadership based on stakeholder actions (or lack thereof). They allow you to know when it's time to inspire with a vision update based on milestones achieved on the project plan and when individual stakeholders or groups need a dose of encouragement from you. Your relationship orientation toward leading people brings more humanity into the tasks to be done, as overseen by your project manager.

## Developing and Influencing People (Your Business Change Lead)

While your project manager handles tasks, your dedicated business change lead focuses on relationships with stakeholders and the delivery of change activities such as communications and training (aka the lower half of the model). This individual serves as your trusted relationship lieutenant and provider of insights into the people side. When you select a business team member for this temporary role strategically for professional development, they gain valuable skills by participating in the change in this way. This person leverages existing relationships to influence behaviors at a peer level.

The business change lead doesn't have to be a subject matter expert in change or specific business processes and technology. Their lack of expertise often helps them ask necessary naïve questions, such as "Why do we do it this way?" and "How should we share this information?" They do, however, need to seek out experts when they need help.

Your business change lead needs to show two strengths:

1. **They have "street" credibility with their peers (aka your team).** Trustworthy and reliable, this individual helps others even when something is outside their expertise.

2. **They possess relational influence.** They're willing to advocate for the change using their relationships. They model new behaviors for their peers, and

their peers seek them out for help. They listen to feedback and actively share it with you and the project manager so that you can adjust.

This temporary role should be staffed by an internal team member rather than a consulting partner or change management professional. However, your business change lead may require support from outside experts. It is usually a part-time role, depending on the complexity of your stakeholders. It's essential to the long-term sustainment of the change that at least one person other than you understands all the behaviors that need to change so that they can continue supporting and influencing their peers after the experts leave.

When your core change team operates with discipline and role clarity about how to approach the change, you significantly reduce the complexity and anxiety you feel about what you're supposed to do and who does it. You show others that the change is doable when you break it into smaller parts and work together effectively in managing tasks and leading people. When you start with a long-term focus on people, you more clearly and convincingly answer the question of "Why are we doing this?" with credibility and authenticity. View the online tool kit on page 17 for a version of this model that includes role descriptions.

## Cera Day's Story

Cera Day finishes her weekly project team meeting and begins crafting her recognition notes. During the team discussion, she gathered insights from Sergio, her project manager, and Athena, her business change lead. They highlighted James, one of her workstream leads, who's helping the team with business process design. James demonstrated courage by asking questions during the technology demo and even shared his screen to do an impromptu demo during the meeting. He carefully walked through the business process so that his peers could see how things were changing. James was initially apprehensive about taking on the role, let alone facilitating discussions with peers.

Cera writes:

> James,
>
> Thank you for courageously leading the team discussion around business process changes! Your willingness to step in even when nervous shows your commitment to helping your colleagues. You prepared well to answer questions and did an excellent job patiently explaining things. I know many answers still need to be determined, but this got us off to a great start in providing more clarity around the change. You set an example for others. Thank you!
>
> — Cera

Cera stops typing and notices she's smiling. She feels excited and hopeful as she writes these notes each week and discusses accomplishments with Sergio and Athena. She wants it to be a regular practice of encouraging efforts to help the team grow. The three of them are settling into a rhythm of managing the tasks and leading people. Adding Athena to the team brought a huge relief and allows Cera more time to focus on the vision and overseeing things holistically. Athena's stepping into the business change lead role with positivity, which encourages project team peers like James to take more risks as they learn. Athena's willingness to opt in got the ball rolling for others.

Cera is diligent about rewarding those choices each week through her recognition notes.

Cera has noticed a shift in the team's energy, as there are more questions during staff meetings and a general interest in what's happening within the project team. As James shared the process maps, Cera sat back to observe the group. Manuel watched the presentation rather than hiding in his laptop. Maria's body language showed openness rather than her usual scowl.

During these sessions, Cera also noticed the team using the word *we* when they talked. The broader team doesn't see the change as separate; they feel like they're part of it and influence decisions with their feedback. As James spoke about the business process steps, the questions remained respectful. A natural back-and-forth ensued as they clarified what James knew and what remained undecided. Manuel even called out how much James has grown. Appreciation from a peer in front of the group means as much to James as this note from Cera will.

The team believes this will help them grow. Although technology is a tool, it's still about them. They can tangibly see and feel what it means to put people first.

*Can we do this? We ARE doing this. Why are we doing this? For our team.* Cera feels the relief of believing the probability just got stronger.

## *One Small Shift:*
## A WHY THAT'S MORE POWERFUL THAN FEAR

Let's be honest: There's a good reason for doubt at the start of a change, particularly when your organization has a poor track record with past changes. Ambiguity and uncertainty are at their highest early on.

You start removing that doubt when you reduce the complexity of implementing the change using the Human-Centered Change Model, which clearly defines your role and the support you receive from your project manager and your business change lead. By taking direct responsibility for specific tasks and overseeing others through these two key roles, you show your team that you're in it with them. This approach holistically manages tasks and leads people. Together, you become a cohesive, influential core change team. Leveraging relationships during change feels different, too, and that feeling inspires the belief that people are the reason why. It's a belief more powerful than fear.

# People Remember How You Made Them Feel

Fear keeps us focused on the past or worried about the future. If we can acknowledge our fear, we can realize that right now we are okay. Right now, today, we are still alive, and our bodies are working marvelously. Our eyes can still see the beautiful sky. Our ears can still hear the voices of our loved ones.

– Thich Nhat Hanh

# 5

# AM I STRONG ENOUGH?

*Managing Your Energy*

## A Note from the Author

The physiological, psychological, and emotional load expected during a transformational change is enormous. Fear takes a toll on your nervous system, particularly if you don't notice it happening. Over time, the body remains on alert, worried about what will happen next, and stress accumulates.

I have learned what happens when you try to ignore and deny fear. It's not gone; it's just building up until it shouts to be heard (sometimes literally). Nervous system overload has happened numerous times for me; and when it does, even the simplest of decisions becomes difficult. My mind can't focus. Soft skills that usually come easily deteriorate. I snap sharply and impatiently, often with mixed signals from a cluttered mind. Tears can surface quickly. My upper chest and throat become tight, and my voice becomes shaky as I talk. Even sleep doesn't bring relief. The underlying nervous feeling persists until I am willing to name it: I feel worried. I feel apprehensive. I feel uncertain. I feel afraid.

Managing my nervous system to prevent overload is not unlike how we prevent other types of diseases and ailments. It's a habit, like eating healthy, exercising regularly, and getting enough quality sleep. The habit of noticing fear as it's happening helps to address it in the moment rather than letting it persist in your body. It's taken me practice to notice my body's sensations, but those have now become my clearest signal to pause.

This short chapter serves as an intermission to remind you to take care of yourself to prevent your version of overload and burnout. **Mindfulness** techniques are proven methods to help you stop worrying about the future and return to the present moment. These practices are easy and quick, allowing you to use them at work even during high-stakes and high-stress situations. Regular practice strengthens the neural pathway that shifts your brain out of reactive fear. You can also practice this when you're in a relative state of calm. Do it enough times, and you will support yourself in preventing nervous system overload so that when fear does arise, you'll be faster at shifting.

## Notice Sensations Using Body Scanning

One upside of intense fear is that it can help you notice where it exists in your body more quickly. **Body scanning** is a mindfulness technique that lets you slow down and connect with your physical sensations. You can use it during situations of acute fear. You can also use it as a preventive diagnostic to notice how fear may accumulate in your body in the form of physical symptoms such as recurring headaches, a backache, or tight neck and shoulders.

Check in with yourself right now using a body scan with these steps:

1. Find a quiet place where you will not be distracted for five minutes. Sit comfortably.
2. Begin focusing on your natural breathing rhythm. Connect with each breath as it flows in and out.
3. Starting at the top of your head, focus on each body part to notice any sensations in your head. Are they strong or subtle? Persistent or fleeting? Does it feel numb or absent of sensations? Is it comfortable or uncomfortable?
4. Slowly progress down your body, moving from your head to your neck, shoulders, core, arms (even your fingertips), back, hips, and legs, down to the tips of your toes.
5. Your job is not to change the sensations but to notice them. Try to stay observant for several minutes, breathing comfortably and consistently.

After completing the body scan, notice how you feel physically, including areas where you may be holding on to tension. A successful practice highlights discomfort in your body to bring more compassion and care to yourself. A body scan forces your mind to slow down. A five-minute investment could save you from (literal) headaches that would otherwise keep you from being calm and clear-minded.

## Releasing Stress Through Breathwork

So long as you live, you breathe. Returning to this rhythm is another way to bring your mind to a more neutral state that's focused on the current moment, rather than worrying about the future or longing for the past. No matter where and when worry strikes, noticing your breath can bring you back to the present.

Body sensations or intrusive thought patterns are clues to reset yourself with deliberate breathing. To do this, pause, inhale through your nose for a count of four, and exhale through your mouth for a count of eight, concentrating on the air flowing in and out of your lungs as you do so. The extended exhale is a signal to release whatever you're worrying about. Repeat this for several minutes until you feel body sensations reducing.

**Breathwork** helps calm down racing thoughts and return you to what remains constant: your breath, here and now. Its many techniques support a variety of intentions. Your breath can calm down and clear out unpleasant thoughts as well as energize and amplify pleasant ones, such as optimism and strength. The releasing breath technique shared in this section helps you recover in the moment, while other breathwork techniques can be used as a preventive practice within your daily routine. This is an excellent tool that's subtle enough to be used in high-stress meetings. No one but you will even know you're doing it.

## Getting Outside

Getting outside in awe-inspiring nature helps you reconnect with sensations in the moment. You see the bright blue sky or lush greenery rustling in the breeze, hear birds chirping and darting between branches, and even feel the touch of pesky mosquitoes buzzing around and landing on your skin. A regular mindfulness practice of getting outside to notice natural sensations returns you to presence by noticing what you feel, see, smell, and hear. This particularly grounding exercise is helpful during times when uncertainty and impermanence feel pervasive.

Getting outside reduces anxious feelings. Try a specific technique of noticing objects around you to reset your racing mind. Name the color and the object in nature, such as green grass, blue sky, brown tree, or white cloud. The ***object and color naming technique*** forces your mind to slow down. You can use this naming technique even when you're stuck inside using the same idea: black desk, brown chair, white wall. Do this for a couple of minutes until your mind resets.

*One Small Shift:*
## PREVENTING BURNOUT THROUGH MINDFULNESS

Mindfulness can be used to prevent the buildup of fear and calm yourself in the moment. Creating a daily habit of using mindfulness techniques such as body scanning, breathwork, and getting outside will build muscle memory in your brain so that when you experience fear, you immediately notice it and use a mindfulness technique that works for you. These habits will help you care for your nervous system like you would for other aspects of your health. Caring and compassion toward yourself will help you feel more powerful when fear appears in your life. Just remember that you can do something to help yourself feel better.

# Emotions Influence Behaviors

# 6

# WHAT'S NEXT ON THIS EMOTIONAL ROLLER COASTER?

*Influencing People*

"I have other, more important priorities right now."

"That's not how we do it in our division."

"I miss the way it used to be."

Doubt, frustration, and disappointment dominate every personal interaction and meeting Cera Day attends. There is no more excitement now; her team is intensely experiencing the challenging middle of the change, full of bumps of negativity and twists of complaints.

She rubs her eyes as she feels her energy drop. Her calm exterior hides her physical, mental, and emotional exhaustion. She's digging deep to maintain her poise. This project requires endurance unlike anything she's ever faced, particularly the emotions.

Sometimes Cera feels she can't do it when the helplessness of others gets under her skin. She bristles with irritation at a team member's neediness as they ask the same question again.

Other times, she feels like a pseudo therapist, forced to listen for hours to people griping and complaining without wanting to take ownership of resolving the issue. She shuts people off in those situations.

Cera's support network advises her to keep at it: "It's a marathon, not a sprint." She's not doing anything right or wrong, per se; it's just about staying with it. There are several months left in the project, and the mountain of work continues piling up.

Cera tries to recall a friendly face. Who can she turn to for support and encouragement? It's lonely out front. When the emotionally charged questions come at her, she sees the distance between herself and others. Her determination helps her keep going, but other team members don't possess the same willpower. So many of them are now stretched to their capacity and ready to give up. Is it impossible?

Everyone wants the same thing: to feel good again. Cera wants that for her team. She wonders, *How can we possibly get through this? How can I help them without burning myself out? How long until we get there? Does anyone see the upside yet? What's next on this emotional roller coaster?*

## Accepting Emotions

How do you feel about roller coasters? Do you seek them out? Or vehemently avoid them? Change is a roller coaster. Now that you're on it, you can embrace the ups, downs, twists, turns, climbs, and drops. Or, you can spend the entire ride rigidly holding on tight, hating every emotion and sensation you experience.

Remove any uncertainty. Change WILL bring forth all kinds of emotions. You will also experience emotions in varying granularity and intensity levels: anxiety, apprehension, worry, uncertainty, and panic, as examples within the fear category. How you experience emotions will be uniquely you, as will how you'll express them verbally and nonverbally (i.e., through behaviors). That can feel chaotic for a leader trying to make sense of all of it for themselves and their team.

You may be fearing the emotions in yourself and how to talk about them productively as you witness emotions in others. It's natural to avoid what feels unpleasant. Learning ways to lean into emotions by influencing them will help you shift out of that fear to feel more confident. Most leaders arrive in their roles with little or no education about emotions, yet that education is vital for leading during change. Armed with knowledge from recent breakthroughs in the science of emotions, you can dramatically impact your capability to adapt to change and accelerate your team's adoption capabilities. Emotions influence behaviors; what we *feel* influences what we *do*.

Neuroscientist and author Jill Bolte Taylor has documented how long emotions last: just ninety seconds. That's how long it takes for an emotion to run its course. Basically, choosing to accept an emotion and allow the experience of it—no matter how unpleasant—means that it can dissipate more quickly. Choosing to avoid, ignore, or deny emotions trips the Replay button, which results in the emotion persisting. When you continuously avoid, ignore, and deny, all those unprocessed emotions start to impact your actions. They prevent clear and calm decision-making, which is essential for fast-paced collaboration and dynamic problem-solving. Denying emotions is a recipe for disaster—also known as resistance—whether that's in you or someone else.

One of the things that makes noticing emotions challenging in yourself and others is that there is no universal fingerprint for them. How you express anger is different from another person in another situation. Family of origin and culture significantly shape how we perceive, create, and respond to emotions. For example, Western culture emphasizes more assertive, individual expression of feelings. (You only need to look at political ads to know which emotions dominate culture in the United States.) There are fewer words in English to describe emotional states than in other cultures, some of whom have many ways to describe emotional concepts, such as the cozy, comfortable feeling of simple pleasures that hygge connotes within Danish culture. You learned emotional concepts early in your life, including whether some emotional concepts were to be avoided or cherished. That's how we develop beliefs around pleasant and unpleasant emotions.

Emotional concepts are based on your personal life history. Your brain predicts a reaction based on past experiences, with thoughts and emotions simultaneously leading you to an action. In this way, emotions are not inherent, but rather a social construction heavily influenced by personal context and experience. Understanding this prediction circuit is useful as a change leader because you can interrupt a reaction. By anticipating unpleasant emotions in others, you can design interventions that nudge others away from them and toward positive beliefs and actions.

For example, let's say you anticipate anger from a team member whose responsibilities change. (Which would be a learned, culturally appropriate emotion in the United States.) Rather than avoiding anger, you have a one-to-one direct conversation with this person. Noticing and naming the anger during the conversation diffuses it. You're ready in the moment to nudge the individual toward a choice you've designed.

Let's say you're asking this person to teach a colleague how to do a certain responsibility going forward. You, of course, thank them for contributing, which shifts an unpleasant feeling into a positive belief: "I'm helping others by sharing my knowledge." This nudging technique helps you use emotions to influence behaviors. It makes dealing with emotions less scary, since you realize you're not trying to control everything but to influence what you can, gently and consistently.

## Anticipating Emotions

The BIG roller coaster at the amusement park is leading a large change project with more intense twists, turns, drops, and climbs. Your prediction circuit is likely anticipating fear. The ride gets less scary when you know what's coming.

Picture yourself walking up to the ride. The other patrons who are waiting are chatting animatedly, with a mixture of anticipation and nerves. As the previous riders enter the station, they display high energy as they get off the ride. They talk expressively about what they remember and feel in detail, all the highs and lows. The faces of some riders relax as the coaster pulls into the station, conveying a sense of relief that the adventure has ended. Others head back immediately to the line to ride again.

You pull one of those riders aside and ask, "So how was it? What should I expect?"

## What's Next on This Emotional Roller Coaster?

Her answer? "Things start slow in the beginning. There's a brief climb up a small hill. We paused at the top, and I got to look down and see the steep, steady drop coming. I felt *nervous* and *excited*. I had butterflies in my stomach. The cars slowly crested the summit, and while I braced myself expecting us to drop fast, it was slow and controlled. That was *irritating*.

"Then, as we reached the bottom of the drop, we leveled out and chugged along for quite a while. This section felt like being thrown around in a washing machine. I disliked this part the most. It felt like slogging through mud; it was long, tedious, and *frustrating*. Then we slowly started heading back up, and up, and up! I felt the butterflies again. That was *fun*! Finally, we were back here, safe and sound."

If you asked 100 riders about their experiences, you'd get 100 different answers. They would all use different words to describe how they experienced the ride, both in terms of physical sensations and emotions. It's not about trying to anticipate or unwind every person's experience. It's about finding commonality that you can use in designing change activities. There are ways to generalize the experience. Namely, the roller coaster feels like an emotional drop from where you start to a low point; and hopefully, if you design change and influence behaviors effectively, you'll climb back up to an endpoint that's higher than the start.

These three points represent the peak experience moments during change. These points are what you are nudging toward. The experience feels like a roller coaster, but if it were represented as straight lines between these three points, it would look more like a check mark:

## Emotional Checkmark Change Journey

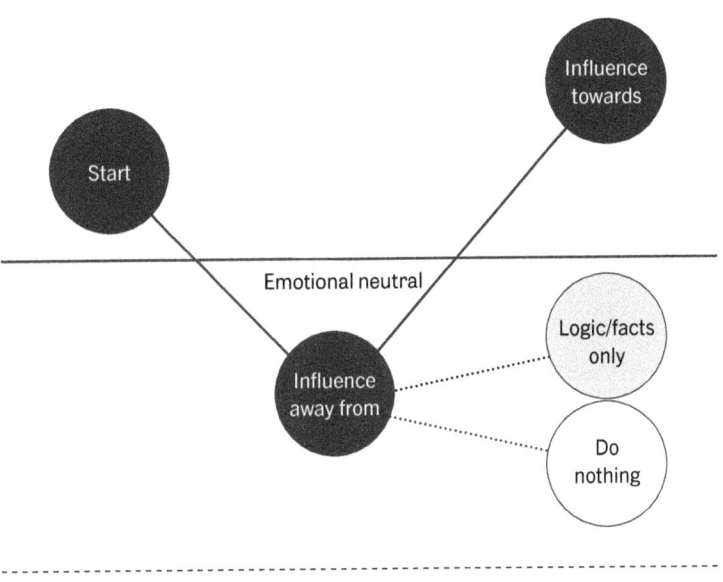

*Figure 4*

By anticipating that your team will reach an emotional low and that you want to climb back up toward the pleasant high, you can design interventions that help this happen more quickly. Your actions to influence emotions at the low point and the pull you create through rewards help support the climb back upward. Also, note that if you do nothing or use only logic and facts, you prolong the time spent in the unpleasant emotions of fear, disgust, anger, and sadness. These emotions cannot be completely avoided, but you can influence how long they last and whether you hit the Replay button to create persisting resistance.

## Using the 3N Influencing Technique

Some organizations downplay or discount emotions, believing they don't belong in the workplace. After all, skipping them helps work go faster, right? But just the opposite happens during change. People get stuck and can't learn new knowledge and skills because they can't go through what Elisabeth Kübler-Ross describes as the natural grieving process, represented as a change curve.

Getting stuck in an emotion creates resistance to the change. However, resistance can be easily prevented by **noticing** and **naming** emotions, followed by **nudging** behaviors once emotions subside. The 3N Influencing Technique helps you connect emotions with behaviors. You first saw how to apply this technique to yourself in chapter 1 to nudge yourself out of reacting and into responding when you notice fear. Now we'll look at how to use it with others as well.

The 3N Influencing Technique provides an easy-to-implement practice based on applying behavioral science to the temporary nature of emotions. This technique is used when you want to shift away from unpleasant emotions—fear, disgust, anger, or sadness—and when you want to move toward pleasant emotions, including various granularities in the happiness category. It supports nudging unproductive mindsets and behaviors into more positive ones. The consistent use of this technique also helps you create an environment with clear expectations of handling emotions appropriately at work by responding rather than reacting.

This technique allows you to fluidly respond in the moment by:

1. **Noticing the Emotion:** It may be nuanced, such as grief mixed with anger; or it may be masked, such as anger hiding fear. Noticing isn't about precision; it's simply a clue to pause. Reassure the other person, "Let's take a minute to slow down."
2. **Naming the Emotion:** Operate from a place of connection. Naming encourages accepting the emotion rather than trying to control it. People will describe their feelings differently. There are no right or wrong words, but talking about emotions normalizes them to help you find common ground with the other person. Ask a gentle question such as, "I sense some sadness. Is that accurate?"
3. **Nudging into Response Mode:** Through the first two steps, you allow the emotion to subside. (It takes just ninety seconds, after all.) Now, you will nudge into response mode for calmer, more collaborative problem-solving to occur: "I hear you. Now that you've shared your feelings, what do you choose to do?" Offering the behavioral nudge as a choice allows the person to shift into hero mode by letting them decide what action to take. Let's look at nudging in more detail:
   a. **After noticing and naming the emotion**, ask, "Is there more to how you feel?" The other person's response will tell you if the emotion has subsided.
   b. **If the other person's emotional cycle has been completed,** here's an example of how they may answer: "No, I was just frustrated for

a bit." When you respond, repeat the language they used about their emotion, which affirms that you see how they feel: "Thank you for sharing your frustration. I can understand why you felt that way. You paused to notice it and shared it productively. Now, let's talk about what to do next."

c. **If the other person's emotion persists**, here's an example of how they may respond: "I'm frustrated that this issue keeps coming up." Give yourself and the other person more time to shift. Observe and ask them to reflect: "I know it feels discouraging right now, and I see you are frustrated. Let's take a break and return to it in a few days. Between now and then, when you feel calm, write down the support you need. We can discuss how I can help when we meet again." Following through and revisiting the topic at the subsequent meeting is essential to close the emotional cycle and move into response mode.

The 3N Influencing Technique addresses emotions in the moment instead of letting them fester. Taking two minutes to do this prevents resistance that can last exponentially longer.

## Influencing Your Boss Out of Fear

Let's show what the 3N Influencing Technique looks like in various emotionally charged situations for Cera Day, starting with this interaction with her boss, Sophia.

"The CFO is questioning why we're doing this project," says Sophia pointedly during their regular update meeting. "It's a big capital investment that, on paper, doesn't appear to support our customer focus strategic priority this year. I don't have a good answer for her."

Cera detects a strong emotional undertone in Sophia's voice. She pauses to *notice* her boss's body language: furrowed brows, a frown, and crossed arms as she sits in her chair, leaning back just slightly. These are subtle clues of anger, and possibly some fear.

Cera wants to get the fear out in the open. She confirms which emotions are present with a question: "I imagine you feel doubtful. Is that accurate?"

Sophia's face softens and shows surprise at the question. She's not used to people asking her about her emotions. But she and Cera have built a strong rapport over many years of working together. Cera simultaneously *named* the primary emotion—fear—and diffused the situation.

"Yeah, I hadn't *noticed* it," Sophia answers. "I do feel uncertain, but also frustrated because I thought we were past the stage of asking why we were doing this project. Did I not do a good enough job of making our case early on? Perhaps I rushed through this topic with the executive team." Her body language relaxes.

Cera believes Sophia has completed the emotional cycle, as she's not showing the fear or anger she was just a minute ago. She pauses a bit longer, then completes the cycle by *nudging* with a question: "What support do you need from me?"

"Do you have some slides I can share?" Sophia responds. "We have the business case to refresh the CFO's memory."

"Is it about the numbers?" Cera asks.

INSPIRED BY FEAR

"No, but it's how we'll start the dialogue by speaking to her in her language."

"I'll pull a few things together for you by Monday," Cera says, closing the discussion.

### Nudging Out of Fear

Managing upward through intense emotions requires delicate maneuvers. Generally, you will deliver your questions, comments, and nudges with more deference. The naming step will be observations; nudges will feel more like suggestions to respect hierarchy.

In Western culture, it's common for leaders in positions of authority to mask vulnerable emotions such as fear or sadness with anger. In this example, Sophia's body language provides clues about her strongest emotion (fear), and she readily admits her frustration (anger). Her strong self-awareness and trusting relationship with Cera make it possible for Cera to nudge her into responsive action in the moment.

When leaders continue to show anger, they're not yet in a win-win frame of mind. It's a clue that more processing must happen first. In a similar conversation with your boss, calling on your patience will be incredibly important to revisit the topic after the anger subsides. You want to complete action-planning with a clear mind and a neutral emotional state.

## Influencing a Peer Who's Angry

The conversation with the CFO helped Cera and her boss, Sophia, reach the source of some feedback about the project: Rowan, a sales manager who attended one of the demonstration sessions. Rowan shared his thoughts with his boss, who relayed them to the CFO, who then paraphrased the comments to Cera: "This project is putting more work on managers like me. I don't have time to do this. My sales team needs to be selling. This is HR's responsibility, and they're pushing it onto us."

Even without being directly involved in the conversation, Cera notes Rowan's evident anger. Providing details on the business case won't address this concern. It's also not an issue between Sophia and the CFO. Rowan is Cera's peer, so she must manage the relationship. She invites her business change lead, Athena, to join her for a discussion with Rowan.

Cera opens the meeting with Rowan empathetically: "I hear your frustration, and I understand why you may think that doing the tasks in the system seems like it'll take more time. At first, it probably will."

Rowan's expression changes from a scowl to a smirk. He's surprised. He'd come into this meeting ready for a battle.

Cera *notices* this and quickly *names* it with a lighthearted comment: "Have I surprised you with my candid honesty?" She smiles playfully. Athena's soft laughter reinforces the gentle approach to building rapport. They're not here to demand compliance from him.

Rowan chuckles and lets his guard down. "Yes, it's refreshing. And honestly, it'll save us a lot of time if we can agree this isn't my job or a good use of time for my sales team." His firm, confident tone suggests he is used to getting what he wants and is not yet ready to talk collaboratively.

Cera seeks more details to clarify his position. "I understand why you may be frustrated in anticipation of how things will shift. As you participated in that system demo we held to gather input, I'm curious about your first impressions?"

"I guess I don't know what I think yet," Rowan states. "Everything happened so fast, and it was hard to follow along." He looks down and away from Cera and Athena. Perhaps he's a bit embarrassed.

"That's helpful feedback," Cera responds softly to show she's receptive, not defensive. She proceeds slowly to give him time to process the emotion. "We'll work to slow down the pace of our future demos. Would you meet with me one-to-one to walk through it again more slowly? I'd love to know where you get stuck and which things you think will take the most time."

"Sure. If you can find thirty minutes on my calendar, please schedule something." Rowan now shifts back into a more assertive stance.

Cera ends the first meeting here, as it reflects good progress. She sets up another meeting with Athena and Rowan the following week to repeat the demo for him.

During the next meeting, Cera begins, "Thank you for meeting with us again today. It'll help us better help you—and, ultimately, all managers. That's why we're doing these demos with a small group early: so we can learn before we roll it out to the entire organization."

Athena leads the walk-through of the system step-by-step, as she is more familiar with the navigation than Cera. But Cera watches Rowan closely to ensure he sees every click Athena makes. She even repeats some of the critical navigational clicks that, as a manager, he will regularly do in the system.

Cera can see that much of Rowan's frustration stemmed from getting overwhelmed with the unfamiliar layout of the system. She notes that she will talk with Athena about slowing down during future demos and repeating steps multiple times so that employees can absorb them better. Together, they have *nudged* Rowan into a more collaborative response by listening to his emotions, which provided valuable opportunities for improvement.

By the end of the demo, Rowan is more relaxed and shares his opinions in even more detail: "I'm just one manager. Plenty of people would be better at this technology stuff. I've been around long enough to know these fancy, new-tech toys show up with big promises of how they will improve my job. But they never do, and so I wait it out. Besides, I like working with my Ops rep, Penney. She does a good job whenever we need to hire someone, and I enjoy talking with her. We don't have enough of that human-to-human interaction around here anymore."

Cera asks Rowan to continue sharing feedback with her. He agrees. Cera and Athena both thank him, knowing that this feedback will significantly improve their future demos and how they communicate system benefits to managers.

**Nudging Out of Anger**

Many people shy away from investigating angry feedback. Your goal as a change leader should be to run toward the fire, not away from it. A manager who's brave enough to share candid comments may represent a canary in the coal mine. Spending more time with this one person can prevent negative feedback and resistance from a much larger group of stakeholders.

Taking a long-term, patient approach in her nudges gives Cera a valuable source of ongoing input. If she can gain Rowan's trust by applying the 3N Influencing Technique, he can become an advocate in future meetings with peers throughout the organization. With your peers, having a little fun and listening to feedback can go a long way in connecting with them. It can also be helpful to have another team member such as your business change lead in a feedback session such as this so you can compare observations and work together to nudge the stakeholder.

## Influencing a Team Member Who's Sad

"Remember before the acquisition, when things were simple? I miss those days."

Cera listens as Penney, a member of her Ops team who supports regional managers, speaks. Penney recounts nostalgically how work felt a few years ago before the company completed a large acquisition that nearly doubled the organization's size.

Cera can relate to her sentiment; her job is immensely different now, with team members in multiple states. She used to be able to walk down the hall for face-to-face conversations. Online touchpoints replaced those conversations, given her time and distance constraints in managing twice as many people spread out in different locations.

This significant change she's leading intends to solve some of the acquisition's challenges. Everyone on the same system will improve operational efficiency while signaling to employees that they're on one team. Cera strives to keep past perspectives in mind when she's talking to various team members who relate differently to how things "used" to be.

As Cera observes Penney, she notices her slouched body language and downcast eyes. "It's different now, isn't it?" Cera asks rhetorically. "I never imagined how things would change, and I didn't appreciate what we had before. Our close-knit team was a special thing we had together. I am sad about losing that, too." Cera *notices* and *names* Penney's emotions by sharing hers.

Penney relaxes in her chair. She visibly exhales to signal

her relief. She wants a moment for someone else to listen and understand her grief.

Cera maintains eye contact to reassure Penney as she watches the emotion pass. She weaves her mindset *nudge* into the following question: "What is your favorite part of how things work right now?"

Penney's face scrunches up. She looks around the room and shifts in her chair as she considers this big question. Cera gives her ample time to formulate her answer, quietly and calmly watching her without showing any signs of anticipation or rushing through it.

"My favorite part has always been the face-to-face interactions with the people I work with the most," Penney says tentatively, a note of sadness still present—and, perhaps, uncertainty about where the conversation is leading. "The bigger we get, the more impersonal things feel. I feel valuable when I can help someone, and I'm much better at doing that in person."

Cera nods. She notes the similarity in Penney's comments with those from her conversation with the sales manager, Rowan. Underneath the technological change, the culture shifts, too. There's a perception that more technology means less human interaction.

"I can understand why it seems like you might lose that personal touch," Cera says. "Do you believe there's also the possibility it won't be true?"

"Maybe," Penney responds sheepishly. Cera notices that the stress of the transition has accumulated, and Penney adds, "I just don't know anything for sure anymore."

"Do you believe you can make it true?" Cera asks. She's trying to *nudge* Penney into acting to help herself, shifting out of a victim mindset and into hero mode.

"I guess so?" Penney responds, again hesitantly but also more hopefully. She looks at Cera with curiosity about what's coming next.

"Well, I can assure you that you have the power," Cera states confidently, continuing to nudge Penney out of her grief and into action. "Now that I know more clearly what you want your work to look and feel like, I can better help you get there."

Cera closes the conversation by talking about several other work activities. She'll continue nudging after the initial prompt sinks in with Penney about her capability to influence her experience. Yet she's helped Penney feel understood by slowing down to notice and name the emotions.

### *Nudging Out of Sadness*

When nudging a team member, strive to stay in leader-coach mode, focusing on the relationship rather than impatiently seeking to manage the tasks. It takes deep trust and psychological safety to share grief and sadness, which makes your direct reports more likely to share those emotions with you. They also want you to help resolve it. You are showing them how to express their feelings so they can help themselves in future situations without taking on the emotional resolution for them.

You may have to repeat your noticing and naming steps, as the masking emotions of fear and anger can hide sadness. Your team member likely needs more time to acknowledge the grief, since it can bring deep vulnerability. When you do, you create an opportunity for a magical moment to empower that individual out of victim mode and into becoming a hero of their own story through action, as Cera attempted to do with Penney. This is a professional victory, but personal growth is also coming to fruition to help others create the future they want for themselves. This is how an influencing nudge you perform during one change can have a lasting impact on your team for future changes as people learn how to own their emotions and actions.

## Influencing for Outcomes

Some individuals have a misconception about the purpose of change activities. It's not about making people feel universally happy; it's about changing behaviors, specifically to focus on the people whose behaviors are necessary for the vision to succeed. The intent of this technique is to help influence the emotions of targeted and prioritized stakeholders during the conversations that are most crucial, because the behaviors are most needed for success. Emotions influence behaviors. Those changed behaviors lead to positive emotions, which reinforce the shift.

Strategically, change activities help people find the mindset to adopt new behaviors, which will then help them feel good about the change. The 3N Influencing Technique supports you in doing that with the stakeholder relationships that are most important to the success of your change, during the conversations where an emotional reaction is preventing you from collaborating or problem-solving. You influence outcomes when you influence emotions.

## Cera Day's Story

Cera Day closes her laptop with a quiet *click*. She lets out a long exhale to release the stress of the long day, then begins packing her bag to head out. As she closes her office door, she notices

## What's Next on This Emotional Roller Coaster?

the quiet and solitude. Yet she feels far from alone and isolated as she once did. She's working diligently on staying connected with others through the challenges, starting with noticing and naming emotions.

A few weeks ago, it felt as if Cera was carrying an enormous weight of emotional labor. She treated emotions as problems to avoid and other people as the enemy. Now, she's learning to catch herself in "me versus you" thinking, which led to her feelings of isolation. Ironically, by focusing on relationships over tasks in emotional moments, she's finding more traction and satisfaction.

Listening carefully during these emotional conversations has led to better task delivery. The feedback has revealed patterns about hidden risks of the change. Cera has been so focused on the future and trying to explain what's changing that she lost sight of honoring what's working in the current environment. Managers appreciate the personal support from Ops reps like Penney. If those two groups partner together to help each other during the rollout, they'll smooth out the bumps. Cera has also preempted a potentially significant issue by realizing the slow, deliberate training methods some stakeholder groups need, since many employees aren't tech-savvy. She guesses they need hands-on help through trusted relationships rather than written instructions that they'll be too frustrated to read.

Uncovering this potential risk through her conversations with Rowan could become the single point of failure on the people side of the project. Cera and Athena, her business change lead, have now shifted more effort toward preparing these stakeholder groups and changing how they deliver the training, with more in-person support between managers and their Ops reps.

Leaving work feels more satisfying now because Cera knows she's made a difference to her team and others. Facing emotions head-on rather than ignoring the anger, grief, and fear feels different from past changes. She feels more capable; and in connecting with others, she realizes she's not alone. She thinks, *We're doing this hard thing—together.*

*One Small Shift:*
## ACCEPTING EMOTIONS TO INFLUENCE BEHAVIORS

Becoming an effective change leader requires accessing more than cognitive intelligence. It also requires emotional literacy, awareness, intelligence, and influence. Emotions help you relate to and influence your team on a level beyond logic. It enables you to operationalize the Human-Centered Change Model introduced in chapter 4.

Leading change allows you to build muscle memory in these skills around emotions. There's ample opportunity to practice recognizing emotions, naming them, and using influential nudges to release them. With practice at accepting emotions, you'll improve your capability to influence behaviors. This is a powerful skill for navigating difficult situations and making you a more influential change leader.

# Conversations Build Teams

# 7

# IS ANYONE LISTENING?

*Building Relationships Through Conversations*

Cera Day looks around the room during her monthly team meeting. Her project manager, Sergio, focuses on his laptop, intensely concentrating on a task. Manuel stares at his phone. Other team members continue entering the room quietly even after the meeting starts, avoiding eye contact and slipping into seats without greeting their peers. This update intends to keep Cera's team informed about what's happening on the project.

Everyone complained about past projects not communicating enough, so Cera and Sergio added this activity to the communications plan. As Cera looks around the room now, she notices everyone else's glazed-over looks as Sergio begins sharing the status update.

The team looks as if they'd rather be at the dentist, getting a cavity filled.

Cera begins tap-dancing under the table—again. She wiggles to let the anxious energy out. She's anything but bored, and she's frustrated at the lack of engagement. She desperately wants her team to realize what's coming, as their success leads to the project's success. Some of this team will be stretched to capacity to grow their skills. She's getting it . . . but they're not.

While she tries to hold on to empathy, Cera feels her frustration kicking in. *This update is just noise,* she thinks. *Why do I even bother?* Her anger escalates as she realizes how much work she and Sergio put into communicating, yet it doesn't appear to make an impact. Communication always comes up on the feedback surveys about what she can do better. She's trying, but nothing works.

*Maybe it's not them. Perhaps it's me.*

Cera doubts her communication capabilities suddenly. *Have I fallen into project speak? Am I using too much of the consultants' jargon? Is anything I'm saying getting through to people? Do they understand why we're doing this and its importance to our future?*

*Hello out there. Is anyone listening?*

## Cultivating Conversations

In an era of information overload and competing priorities, focusing on generating awareness of change through distributing broad-based communication materials alienates people with more noise. That is, if they're reading anything at all. Understanding happens in discussions via relationships, where dialogue creates meaning around possibilities of what could be better, and ideas and empathy are exchanged. Information-oriented status updates tell your team what work comes next, but they don't influence their hearts so that your team feels good about the vision and commits to new ways of working.

The Human-Centered Change Model (see chapter 4) requires you to equally manage tasks and lead people. Let's clarify a core activity that happens during change and the difference in intent it has on each side of the model. Communications inform, which makes them task-oriented. Conversations engage and inspire, which makes them people-oriented. Conversations use more emotion and listen more. Your core change team collaborates across both kinds of activities, using feedback to adjust and improve. But within the model, there are certain activities that are best delivered by you.

In chapter 6, we focused on how to influence during small-group or one-to-one conversations. This chapter looks at conversations that happen in large-group forums, such as team meetings or town halls. In these forums, you facilitate the conversation portion, which requires you to get good at:

- Sharing with more emotion
- Asking great questions
- Listening and responding
- Evolving based on feedback

First, let's address some fundamentals about effective change communications. Every communication serves three functions: how you want people to feel, what you need them to know, and what you want them to do. In the Human-Centered Change Model, emotions matter most. If communication is a three-layer cake, the bottom layer is how you want people to feel. Emotions influence what people know and do. If they're fearful or angry, getting them to learn something or do anything differently will be challenging. Once they do it, you'll also want them to feel good about it. Emotions are the foundational bottom layer *and* the frosting on the cake:

## Emotion-driven Conversations

*Figure 5*

With emotion as the bottom layer and the frosting on the cake, we can now consider how to bring more of that into large-group forums.

## Amplifying Pleasant Emotions

Is any birthday more memorable than one involving a surprise birthday cake, topped with sparkling candles and a custom-crafted picture of you frosted on top? Surprises are one way to amplify desired emotions. You can do this by designing change activities that evoke more pleasant emotions like appreciation, feeling valued, gratitude, curiosity, confidence, and hopefulness. These encourage your team throughout the change, but they are particularly helpful for your team to begin the climb out of the emotional low point when things are the most challenging and frustrating.

Remember, emotions influence behaviors. So the design goal is to amplify specific pleasant emotions by anticipating what your team might experience at critical phases during change. Targeting emotions this way supports the strategic behavioral shifts you're trying to make during that phase. In your role, this can be as easy as adjusting the update you share each month in your department meeting to reflect *how it feels* and *what you want your audience to feel* during the three peak experience moments of the change: the good beginning, the low point of the challenging middle, and the higher, better ending:

1. **The Good Beginning:** "We've started the design process to compare our existing business processes with industry best practices. I'm *confident* that our team will work on the design, as they will take our already good processes and see how we can make them even better. Some of the capable team members leading this work are . . ."

2. **The Low Point of the Messy Middle:** "I want to recognize our testers, as they work diligently to complete more than three hundred test cases. In this testing phase, there are no shortcuts. It's messy but *valuable* and important work. Let's show some *appreciation* for our testers. Thank you to . . ."

3. **"Something Better" at the End:** "I'm *grateful* for those of you who are learning while helping your business partners through the training rollout. It feels a little overwhelming as the change becomes real. But you are managing it gracefully. Other leaders are sharing examples of how our team is helping their people, including . . ."

This messaging connects *how it currently feels* and *how you want it to feel.* Weaving emotions into recurring updates in your group conversations helps recognition feel more meaningful, and the encouragement lands more fully. You demonstrate that you relate to the team's current emotional state and notice their behaviors. People want to feel good, and when you recognize behavior changes publicly, you encourage more of it. Leaders often believe that being perceived as inspirational requires passionate speeches. In fact, it's the small moments in the regular rhythms of work that offer the easiest improvement for increasing inspiration with your team.

## Asking Great Questions

Curiosity is another emotion that helps cultivate behavior change. You can use curiosity to improve engagement in your group conversations by asking better questions. Rather than asking about things, direct meeting questions toward people and relationships. Notice how subtle changes in language shift from task- to relationship-oriented questions that open doors for more dialogue:

- **When asking questions of presenters:** "I admire your expertise. Can you share more with us?"
- **When directing questions to specific audience members to ensure understanding:** "Athena, what do you see as key differences from how you work with your colleagues today?"
- **When committing to sharing more about a currently ambiguous topic:** "I don't know much

about this, and I feel like there are some experts we could all learn from. Does that interest others?"

- **When asking the group for feedback on future content:** "Who would you like to learn more from next time?"
- **When sharing your aha moments:** "When we reviewed this last week, I learned from my steering committee colleagues that . . ."

Asking questions beyond those that result in a yes or no answer builds the conversational tone even in large-group meetings. Questions that beget questions or comments help people reflect more deeply on a topic, which moves them from passive recipients to engaged participants. When you activate curiosity by asking great questions, you encourage your team to help themselves by removing uncertainty, doubt, and fear. It opens the door for more exploring and self-sufficiency. Doing this early during a change takes the pressure off formal training, allowing knowledge to build gradually over time.

## Listening and Responding

Once you've started asking great questions, building active listening and response skills makes conversations an even more engaging information exchange that gathers feedback to improve. Empathetic listening happens in one-to-one conversations and larger-group formats, such as team meetings.

The first shift is as simple as dedicating more time in your group meetings for listening and feedback. At least one-quarter of the meeting time should be spent listening so that you build trust and psychological safety while allowing the content to evolve more quickly. The cycle of asking and listening in a team conversation looks like:

1. **Opening with a broad yet specific question:** "What's one thing you learned today?" You can then follow up with a request for more details: "What do you want to learn more about next time?"

2. **Responding to emotionally charged questions/feedback instead of reacting:** "Thank you for sharing. I appreciate hearing your perspective. I want some time to consider your comments. Could you schedule time with me to discuss your thoughts in more detail next week?"

3. **Follow up at the next meeting.** Pick up on topics people want to learn more about in future meetings creates a continuous improvement cycle.

Listening and responding feel more like an ongoing conversation that your team can participate in. Learning to operate as a facilitator of conversations in large-group settings helps you build the desired emotions that support behavior change. Listening is also a fundamental element of psychological safety in your culture.

## Inviting Others into the Conversation

Traditional communication methods tend to be structured and rigid. For example, a broadcast email can share information but allows little opportunity to gauge understanding of what's been shared—or even that it's been read. During change, it's important to introduce temporary, new conversation-oriented forums that help people learn from one another, share experiences and tips, and curate empathy. These types of forums help you gauge emotions and check for understanding and behavioral progress. They also evolve based on the needs of the participants.

Your role is less visible in these forums. It is simply your responsibility to dedicate a resource to facilitating them, encourage participation, and remove any barriers to participation such as time constraints for team members. Examples of the distinctions between structured communication formats and fluid conversation forums include:

| Structured Formats (From . . .) | Fluid Forums (To . . .) |
| --- | --- |
| • Formal demonstration | • Choose-your-own-adventure, conversation-style demos (e.g., ask the audience what they want to see) |
| • Required meetings | • Topic-specific office hours taught by peers (e.g., drop in and discuss) |
| • Required training | • Peer mentoring |

Conversation-oriented forums give people a choice to opt in. The group determines where the content goes and how the time gets spent. These fluid forums can be more informal, which requires less preparation. Your business change lead can organize them and track future agenda topics based on feedback. Assigning this engagement activity to your business change lead is a key way for you to guide this individual's development. It's also a primary forum for them to influence their peers. They take the lead on assigning appropriate subject matter experts to share and answer questions as another way of building a coalition of support. The group self-regulates and can always defer a topic to a future session.

Offering these forums as a recurring series allows your team to learn to help themselves as they begin to recognize the value of bringing their questions and getting answers from their peers. These forums should be approachable and relatively informal so that your team members can feel comfortable sharing questions and issues with one another.

## Cera Day's Story

"Last month, we learned a bit about how onboarding will work. Several of you shared that you wanted to know more about how your responsibilities will change. As we reviewed the process and its roles, what do you notice differs from how we work today?"

Cera Day opens the feedback portion of the team meeting with a specific question to acknowledge the input from last month. She looks around the room to notice the concentration in her team members as they formulate their questions. Their eye contact tells her they're engaged and curious. She's learned to pause to give them time. However, they're still somewhat ambivalent about taking the lead to ask the first question. If necessary, Cera has prompted Athena to step in to start the sharing. Cera stands at the front of the meeting room, still and quiet, trusting that one of her team members will speak up.

It's taken a few rounds, but each demonstration cycle has led to more engagement in asking questions or sharing opinions. It helps Cera know that her team "gets it." They're not sitting back, waiting for directions. Instead, they're showing their interest. Ironically, talking too much and sharing too much information made Cera feel unheard. The silence reflected that the information overload added to the fear. Now, she's more planful in considering the emotions and questions she wants to cultivate each time she talks with her team. Today, she's trying to encourage curiosity with her question prompt.

Sometimes, the conversational format takes the team off-topic. Last month, it opened the door for an impromptu recognition of Manuel, who recently finished a professional certification he'd been working toward for several years. In the past, Cera would have been annoyed by this. Now, Cera feels patient and hopeful because it symbolizes the camaraderie being built in the team. She knows that it's essential that they all look to one another for help and encouragement, rather than always asking her.

Their core change team is also working together more effectively. Coordinating with her project manager, Sergio, and her business change lead, Athena, alleviated some of Cera's pressure about poor communications feedback. It doesn't all rest on her. Sergio and Athena take the lead on the facts, such as project accomplishments and what's coming next that needs to be done, while Cera makes that come to life with stories of how the changes will improve their work life. Athena's also taken the lead on getting others involved in leading demonstrations and answering questions. Each week, when they meet, they talk about feedback and confirm future topics. It's a tag team effort, and they've built a cohesive rhythm that they adjust based on feedback and observations.

Cera pulls up the final slide in the meeting's presentation deck. She beams with pride and appreciation as she recognizes team members. They're in the challenging middle of the project, and she knows that specific encouragement goes a long way toward the team continuing to learn. As she highlights team members for their contributions, the smiles and congratulations from their peers lift the entire group's mood. It feels like they're celebrating together each month and ending on a high note.

It felt scary at first to bring more heart into Cera's team communications, as no one else talked this way in her organization. But she does it because she knows it feels better for her and her team. She's seeing the impact of those feelings in the changes in their behaviors, too.

## *One Small Shift:*
## CONVERSING *WITH* PEOPLE

What you say and how you say it matters. Encouraging and recognizing your team inspires them to start and continue new behaviors. The format you choose to build conversations signals to your team that their participation and feedback are important. You converse *with* people, which leads to collaboration and problem-solving. When you facilitate conversations, you influence how your team feels, which gets them curious to learn and, ultimately, increases their desire to do things differently.

When your team feels heard, they share. When your team bravely asks questions that you help answer, they feel safe about asking more questions until they're confident that they understand. When your team seeks clarity on what "better" looks like—and you vividly describe how it feels to get there—you lead them out of the challenging, and potentially demoralizing middle. Conversations build teams.

# Learn as You Go

# 8

# CAN WE LEARN IT IN TIME?

*Learning by Doing*

"Wait, what did you just say?" Adir asks during a planned system demonstration for the team. "I don't understand."

"Well, after you submit the task, you'll want to check on the status by referencing the business process map," the demonstrator explains.

"Business process map?" Adir replies. "What's that? I'm lost. I don't understand what you're saying, and I couldn't keep up with you. When am I going to get trained on this?"

Cera tries to support the situation, which is quickly becoming contentious. "Remember, formal training isn't for a couple more months now. It's right after our go-live."

"What?!" Adir responds frantically. "AFTER going live? I need to know how to do this *before* my business customers do. Otherwise, I will look bad in front of them when they ask for my help! I need training NOW."

*Why do even simple things create such strong reactions?* Cera thinks. She pauses before responding, "I understand why you want to get into the system and see it for yourself. There is a lot to learn. That's why we wanted to show you it first, without you worrying about trying to do it simultaneously."

"I don't get it," Adir says, reacting fearfully. "How am I supposed to do my job? I'll never have enough time to get everything done. I need actual training and step-by-step instructions. This is way too hard."

"Thank you for the feedback," Cera says, wrapping up the conversation with the team. She's not going to solve it in this setting. "We'll regroup to discuss the timing of training and come back to the team at our next meeting with our plan to get more input from you."

As she returns to her office, Cera feels puzzled by the strong reaction the demo caused. It took courage for Adir to speak up. She's glad there's enough trust to share a potentially controversial opinion in front of the group, even if the comments had more anxiety behind them than she feels the topic deserves. There's a lot of fear present.

Still, given the time constraints, the likelihood of training earlier than planned remains low. How can Cera and her team find a way to get more done faster these last few weeks? She'll bring this up at the Project Management Office team meeting for discussion; perhaps her consulting partners will have suggestions.

It feels like a mad dash to the finish, and the training will be the project team's most visible moment to the broader Ops team and the rest of the organization. The emotions present today likely will repeat themselves during those training sessions. Cera knows having a solid plan for the rollout is essential. It's a significant change, and the many new terms and tasks to perform in the system could cause confusion and angst for managers across the organization. She's reflecting on what Rowan has already shown about just how intimidating technology can be for some managers. Her Ops team should know it beforehand, and she knows that Adir's concern is valid. *Is it possible?* Cera thinks. *Can we learn it all in time?*

## Learning Along the Way

The last few weeks leading up to a project launch are frenzied. Many aspects come together at the last minute, including training materials, which depend heavily on other design aspects finishing up. This reality frustrates some team members who seek formal documents ASAP to guide them step-by-step through activities.

Formal training such as instructor-led sessions, self-paced courses, and detailed job aid documentation is only one part of preparing your team. As you learned in chapter 7, other conversation-oriented activities prepare your team for formal training. They will be more ready when they've taken small steps through curiosity-enhancing learning moments before the final butt-in-seat type of learning. (You are going through a similar learning process as you read this book before applying it on the job. You'll be more ready to implement ideas after reading about the concepts.)

The nudging conversations before the final push create readiness to learn. Calm brains are capable of learning. Learning also happens *through* those experiences along the way. Learning is bigger and broader than formal training. For adults at work, learning by doing is the best and most pragmatic way of supporting behavior change. Starting early and taking a holistic approach to learning reduces the pressure during time crunches. It minimizes the risk of depending solely on formal training.

Long before that moment, you build foundational knowledge of the change. This is the context setting and clarity that conversations support, such as knowing how processes and roles are shifting, introducing key terms, and even basic familiarity with any new technology. You also influence hearts and minds to believe in the change, which creates emotional readiness and better conditions for learning. Learning represents the whole picture, not just the how-to steps in the system.

Learning happens every time you involve stakeholders, such as participating in system or process demonstrations, testing, and real-time peer support during on-the-job moments using new skills before and after going live. Research by Robert Eichinger and Michael Lombardo that was shared on the Center for Creative Leadership's blog says 70 percent of leadership learning happens on the job through challenging assignments and experiences. Another 20 percent comes through formal and informal relationships, and only 10 percent happens through formal training, such as courses. Change is one extended learning opportunity for you and your team.

When projects skip involvement activities, training delivered at the tail end becomes a disjointed, frustrating experience for system users who don't believe in the why and lack a basic familiarity with new terms and processes or their role. Pulling forward engagement activities prepares your team for formal training by familiarizing them with activities they'll do in the system. They'll feel more confident because they've repeatedly watched others demonstrate the steps and talked with colleagues about processes and roles. Many of them get hands-on during testing before launch. These learn-as-you-go moments allow your team to practice behaviors to build muscle memory.

Ultimately, change comes down to getting people to *do* things differently, which they'll learn in a detailed how-to way during training. But the deliberate use of moments along the way influences emotions and your team's beliefs. They *can* do hard things so that they're calm and ready to learn them when the time comes.

## Involving Others as Part of Their Learning

Formal training comes last because your project team must work through different possibilities to determine the best solution design options. Redesigning business processes and trying out options takes time to see how things may work for your organization. This is even more complicated if there's technology involved that must be built or customized. It typically takes several rounds before finalization. Only then can formal documentation and delivery happen during training.

Stakeholder involvement sessions during the design and testing rounds support your holistic learning approach. Through an established conversation-style forum, such as technology demonstrations or walk-throughs of process flows, your team gains insights into decision-making and slowly removes ambiguity about what's coming through, showing the work in progress. These sessions leverage two-way discussions to build understanding and shift emotions from doubt into hope. If you are explicit about the sessions serving as early learning, you can also reduce some of the apprehension people feel about waiting until the end for formal training.

These sessions also serve as practice sessions for key team members who may eventually lead formal training, such as your business change lead and other team members leading aspects of the project. Essentially, this approach helps you create trainers. Individuals engage more deeply and meaningfully when involved in designing the solution and gathering feedback. Only some will be naturally effective teachers, but through structure and support, you can design these demonstration sessions as key on-the-job learning moments for the presenter and participants. They are repeatedly practicing new behaviors. These early sessions help prepare your team for formal training later. Helping your team build skills over time through learning experiences such as this takes the pressure off a big-bang approach to training at go-live.

One of the objections frequently raised when proposing these types of demo sessions is, "But the system isn't done yet." That's the point! Letting a broader group of stakeholders see and experience the system before it's finished allows them to come along for the ride. When people get to see "behind the curtain" how the sausage gets made, they feel like they're part of the solution rather than like outsiders. When you set the expectation that these involvement sessions help your team learn alongside the experts early on, you remove the pressure team members feel while waiting for formal training. You influence emotions through this learning approach as people get curious and more hopeful.

One of the ways you can bring visibility to early learning opportunities is by using ***learning goals***. During these involvement sessions, explicitly state, "Today's learning goal is _____." Here are some examples of learning goals:

- Explaining why the team is doing this
- Documenting key roles and role assignments
- Exploring industry best practices such as, "Where are our gaps?"
- Identifying key terms the team needs to know

At the end of the session, ask team members to reflect on the learning goal to identify future content needs. This type of content is a natural way to organize your dedicated conversation-style forums, facilitated by your business change lead with help from subject matter experts.

## Embedding Teachers in Your Team

While using project activities for learning creates growth opportunities for your entire team, the other important aspect is *who* is teaching in these sessions. During the early phases, your team will be in heavy observer-learner mode. They won't yet know the solution and will rely on consulting partners. Ultimately, the goal is for your team to lead these sessions as a marker of their progress in skill development. (You'll know it when you see it. This is one behavior that will tell you whether you're on track early on.)

Learning becomes more purposeful when those team members understand they will eventually be teaching the same material to their peers. Initially, this may sound intimidating for some of your team. But doing it early helps them overcome the hurdle of teaching others long before launch. During team member identification in your project, specifying this teaching responsibility (and selecting for it) helps accelerate the learning, such as more focused listening to learn from consulting partners and clarifying key terms, process steps, or role responsibilities earlier.

This type of teaching approach honors this principle:

> Watch one > Do one > Teach one

After your team has watched the expert consultants navigate tasks, they apply that knowledge to perform the same activities themselves. This prepares them to teach others during subsequent rounds and eventually lead the formal training during project rollout. While training feels like a one-and-done event, learning is ongoing and iterative.

Most project team members expect to be involved in watching and even doing tasks like testing. Many assume the last step—teaching others—will be delegated to a training expert. While this is an option if your organization has trainers ready to support your project, that's not usually the case. It also misses the growth opportunity for your team (remember your why for developing people). It gives them a chance to practice behaviors early on.

By having your team teach others, understanding deepens. Teachers learn to organize their materials and find answers to their own and others' questions. Also, repetition enhances a teacher's confidence in mastering the knowledge. After going live, these individuals become the "go-to" for social support, as colleagues will likely turn to their peers for help first. Having your team be the teachers provides multiple benefits for the change. It role-models adoption, reduces fear by increasing familiarity, and builds confidence through repetitions. This makes your team a safe environment for learning.

Your business change lead is critical to this learning strategy. They coordinate the activities of the various teachers and help them prepare. They model a calm, capable demeanor and respond fluidly to questions. They don't have to be experts on the content. It's OK if they sometimes don't know the details so long as they're an empathetic listener. At this stage in learning, effort is more important than outcome. You want to encourage people to keep trying.

## Formalizing Knowledge Transfer

Consulting experts will likely surround you and your team during a large project. You'll have access to people who have implemented similar changes dozens of times. Yet leaders rarely engage these experts in the learning process for themselves or to formalize *knowledge transfer* with key team members. (You may hear the acronym KT from your consulting partners as shorthand for this.)

You must set expectations with your consulting partners that you want to formalize knowledge transfer activities. This conversation includes you identifying—with their input—three key knowledge transfer areas:

- **What roles** do you want knowledge transfer completed for?

- **How will the knowledge transfer be documented** (e.g., written documentation such as a handbook, teach-backs, video recordings of training sessions)?

- **How long do you have access** to specific consulting experts during *hypercare* (typically, the thirty days following go-live, during which you receive continued support from your consulting partners) in case additional questions or learning needs arise?

Once you agree with your consulting partner on roles, documentation formats, and hypercare duration, add dates for critical handoffs of knowledge transfer documentation into your project plan. A sign-off by your team members verifies their learning needs have been met and ensures accountability from consultants to complete it before they roll off the team and you lose access to their expertise. This approach to knowledge transfer reduces the surprise risk of your team feeling panicked when the consultants depart. They'll know it's coming and prepare for it.

Like other learning, knowledge transfer happens as an ongoing process, with the completion captured through the formal sign-off acknowledgement. Some teams find it easier to review ongoing knowledge transfer as they complete each project phase, ensuring documentation across all workstreams and materials gets loaded to the proper shared reference storage.

Formal knowledge transfer also reduces one of the most common people-related risks on projects: critical roles are ready. You will identify and support the handful of people essential to your project's success based on meeting their learning needs. In other words, they will tell you they're ready based on signing off on the knowledge transfer.

## Measuring Learning Progress

You will also want to measure progress as you build learning into the project activities. The gold standard for measuring adoption is observing new behaviors. You can supplement that with surveys at key milestones.

One caveat about measuring progress: You must be realistic about when you expect to see specific behavior changes in your team. Based on the learning experiences you incorporate into the project, some team members will learn sooner than others. For example, your business change lead, your workstream leads, and other team members serving as teachers will build skills before others who are not as involved (and that's by design). A role-based approach also means you identify the exact behaviors that need to be performed, with individuals assigned to roles. Your behavior-based road map that chapter 4 touched on helps you organize who, what, and when so that you can measure progress using visible behaviors along the way.

Focusing on roles and behaviors helps your team know exactly what they need to learn, when they'll start practicing, and a reasonable timeline for becoming "good" at specific behaviors. Training that's delivered just in time as rounds of repetition on the job makes it more likely for new knowledge and skills to stick. Most of your team will build skills for several months *after* implementing the change. (More about this topic is coming in chapter 9.)

Remember that behaviors are the ultimate measure of successful change adoption. When you know what behaviors are needed for each role, you can measure progress against those behaviors during your practice sessions and testing rounds. In a technology change, the universal behavioral measure is user log-ins: What percentage of users log in within thirty days after going live? A target of 90 percent of the total users indicates users are capable and willing to perform specific tasks for their roles. For power user groups—such as HR, in the case of a new human capital management system—looking deeper at transactions completed can help determine whether your team has adopted using the system as part of their roles. You also clearly know who needs a nudge of some form.

Measuring behavioral progress along the way provides peace of mind that you are working at an appropriate speed toward your end goal. You will feel more confident about your team's readiness because you will see evidence. If you supplement behavioral measures with other types of feedback about learning progress gathered through surveys, you'll know what nudges your team needs. One emotion-focused question will help you gather this input: "How confident do you feel?" Sharing survey results can help you reassure your team members that progress is happening and that you are monitoring it so you can support them. You can even turn it into a celebratory moment, which encourages more learning.

## Cera Day's Story

Cera Day opens her team meeting by acknowledging the previous feedback: "I want to start today's session with a follow-up from our last team meeting when the team asked for training to happen as soon as possible. I understand why you want more training earlier. There's plenty to learn; we haven't always done it well in our past projects. Many of you feel frustrated and maybe even slightly abandoned that we didn't have your backs."

She goes on to say, "I promise you that's not going to happen this time. I will not leave you to fend for yourself. You will be supported throughout this experience. I am committed, and Athena, our business change lead, is committed to ensuring that happens. You also have one another for support.

"Our project team used those past experiences to do things differently in how we support you as learners. Specifically, I'm using the word *learning* to mean a much broader view of how we're supporting you through this transition."

*Learning by Doing*

Cera adds, "Learning is ongoing, and our team needs to know this isn't a one-and-done activity. Formal training may take that format, but learning is bigger than that. It happens on the job and from one another. You all have busy day jobs, so we know that we need to do this bit by bit to keep it manageable. We also need to do it just in time to immediately practice it as soon as we learn to do something. Our testers get to do that earlier, and you will all do it in formal training when the system is finally ready just before you start using it daily.

"With that in mind, I would like to introduce Andrew, who will share a bit about what he has been learning through his role on the project team."

Cera turns the presentation over to Andrew. Athena helped him prepare for the discussion by asking that he share:

- His current learning goals
- Key terms he's learned from his consulting expert
- How he uses a dedicated file he created to document his learning and share it with others
- Who he turns to when he has questions (usually Athena right now)

Cera steps into the background so that Andrew can role-model learning for other team members. His voice reflects confidence. She observes team members taking notes and asking questions. Observing these behaviors tells her the team is owning their learning. They can't—and aren't—waiting for training.

*One Small Shift:*
## LEARNING BY DOING

Learning incorporated into project activities is more manageable for busy teams—and for you, a busy leader. It's why on-the-job, bite-size, just-in-time application strategies are critical to modern workplace learning. It's this type of application that allows your team to know what's expected of them in terms of new behaviors. You can communicate it clearly and measure progress along the way when you take the time to develop a behavior-based road map. A holistic, ongoing approach to learning relieves the tremendous pressure of waiting until the last minute for a big-bang, high-stakes approach to training rollout. It can boost curiosity and confidence when you approach it as a team effort, with learners supporting one another and sharing their aha moments. Start learning earlier, make it ongoing, document accountabilities, and incorporate hands-on activities such as leading demos and testing. Learning is much more than formal training.

The Best Rewards Are
Fast, Easy, and Free

# 9

# IS IT EVER GOING TO END?

*Rewarding Change*

It's been several months since the project went live. While Cera's day-to-day feels mostly back to business as usual, the change doesn't feel "done" for her team.

They're still figuring things out. Is that normal? Shouldn't they be able to do this stuff by now? There have been missed details or low-priority items that got pushed out for later—and later is now. In some cases, more technical development was needed; in others, her team had to create manual work-arounds.

Most of Cera's team needs help keeping up with the pace. They can't do the same amount of work in a regular workday because they're not fast at using the new system and processes yet. It still requires them to think about their actions, rather than perform them automatically. Cera understands the importance of patience, repetition, and encouragement, yet her team shows signs of wearing out. They expected "better" to happen at go-live, but it hasn't arrived yet. There was no spiking the ball as they reached what they thought would be the end zone.

Cera thought the change would be behind them by now,

too. The "tomorrow" she'd been talking about for nearly a year is now "today." Yet it still feels like they're stuck in "yesterday," as people struggle to get used to the new ways of working.

On top of that, the consultants who supported Cera and her team during the development process have left. The safety net of on-call experts to quickly resolve questions and issues disappeared. Even Sergio, her internal project manager, has other project assignments to focus on and limited hours to support the remaining fixes and general system support. Cera knows that's part of managing project costs, but it still leaves her and Athena in a tough spot with responding to the ongoing requests for help. She's grateful that at least she has Athena, who handles many of the blocking-and-tackling-type questions from the team daily.

Her emotions pull her in many directions: frustration and impatience with team members holding on to the past by dragging their feet, hope for those trying to help themselves, and gratitude for those pitching in to help their teammates. She wants to stay empathetic with all of them, yet meeting each person where they're at while maintaining her sanity stretches her emotional endurance.

Cera would love to put it all behind her, but that's not the reality. She doubts that she's been effective in leading this change. It should have been done by now. That apprehension has her asking, "Is it ever going to end?"

## Completing the Transition

As you learned in chapter 2, people success does not happen magically when a change goes live. It happens when the transition to new ways of working is complete. Behavioral measures verify that transition. Even after you finish the activities on the project plan, you will still be nudging (primarily through encouragement and recognition) as your team practices new behaviors.

Success also depends on *feeling* it. Ideally, your team is climbing out of the emotional low point of the change experience to a place that's better than where you started. You're seeing and hearing more positivity. While your personal energy levels may be dwindling, this is another important time to reinforce pleasant emotions like curiosity, hope, optimism, gratitude, and appreciation.

After your go-live but before you reach that point of feeling a completed transition, your efforts depend primarily on what you observe in your team:

- Are they demonstrating new behaviors?
- How consistently are they demonstrating these behaviors?

It took hundreds—if not thousands—of repetitions of the previous behaviors for your team to perform their work without much conscious thought. Immediately after a change, they think about *everything*. Until those new behaviors become second nature, you will want to continue encouraging and rewarding them. Your business change lead and the other teachers embedded within the team will continue teaching and reinforcing the use of support tools such as job aids or process documentation. Those embedded teachers also continue answering questions and talking peers through things that they need help doing.

Individuals master new behaviors with varying speeds, depending on the number of new behaviors for their role(s) and each person's motivation levels. Their desire depends on how effectively you influenced their emotions and shared the rallying cry of the why to build belief in the change. Those conversations you had to clarify processes and roles early and learning by doing all contribute to your success. If you've done an excellent job of igniting intrinsic motivation, people help themselves during this learning phase.

If you didn't nudge to resolve unpleasant emotions earlier, you will observe anger and frustration in more volume and with greater intensity. Your team members who ignored the change or didn't believe it would happen are now feeling those emotions. Others may express grief in longing for what was and say things such as "I was so good at my job before" or "I liked the way we used to do _____." A few of your early adopters, such as your business change lead and teachers, will already want to improve things because they see the possibilities for what's next.

Like they did throughout your change, emotions vary widely during the sustainment phase. Fear is still present in variations like doubt, uncertainty, and apprehension. Many team members will express frustration at you or others if they're in victim mode and want to blame someone for why the learning is difficult for them. You will continue using the skills you gained along the way to influence mindsets, behaviors, and emotions using the 3N Influencing Technique to help people move out of fear, anger, and sadness into a place where they can learn and build confidence. These conversations to gather feedback help you keep improving until you consistently see new behaviors.

Even as your desire to be done is strong, it's important in this phase that you continue:

- Emphasizing the upside of the change

- Finding ways to make the transition fun
- Doubling down on praise, rewards, and recognition
- Refusing to tolerate destructive behaviors
- Highlighting what's next and how it keeps getting better

At this point, you become an astute behavioral observer so that you can intervene on the spot with praise or correction. Your language and behaviors firmly remove doubt about your commitment to seeing the transition through to completion.

## Emphasizing the Upside

After going live, you get to stop talking theoretically and start talking about the new reality. The moment that everyone has been fearing has arrived! For doubters, this quickly shifts their responses. Many people move from disinterest to panic as they try to catch up on what they've been ignoring. Yet others who have been engaging, learning, and growing along the way are starting to experience the upside.

"Better" is no longer a far-off concept of what *might* happen. It is real. You get to begin telling the real stories of what your team is improving and jobs that are becoming easier or better in some way. These stories emerge slowly from your team, usually starting with examples from those who are further along in their mastery. They start sharing excitedly about doing something that they couldn't do before or solving a problem that's bothered them for a long time. Those practical examples of "better" are invaluable stories to share so that they're repeated broadly. This is how new behaviors become more desirable than staying stuck in frustration for those who are still doubtful and fearful. People want to feel good, and those positive examples help overcome resistance.

During the earlier part of the journey, your stories focused on the pain points of what didn't work. The frustration provided a universal villain. Now, more emphasis belongs on the possibilities and upsides of the new capabilities so that your team connects with being the hero in the story. These stories are a lot more fun to tell. But like earlier, using emotions in stories influences behaviors. Lots of positive emotions help new behaviors become stickier faster.

These stories will feature examples of people doing things they couldn't do before, such as serving a customer in a new way. You're facilitating this sharing, even if you're not directly telling the story. Listen for opportunities to invite other voices, such as asking a business partner to share a story during a department meeting, which inspires and encourages your team. Having team members who experienced an aha moment acts as another moment of social proof to influence peers to begin seeing more of the upside. You'll know you've got a good story to share when you hear things like, "Hey, that's cool" or "Wow, I didn't know that." When you hear those things, find out more. Your business change lead can help track down details and is probably hearing other examples, too.

You can also expect some team members to dwell on the negative aspects, such as what's not working yet or the elements of the solution design that didn't adequately capture the business requirements. Keep listening to feedback without fixating on it. Your project manager can communicate details of defect resolution timelines. Your team will experience bumps as they learn, so continuing to talk about wins will balance out the inevitable challenges.

## Making Change Fun

Realistically, energy levels drop at a project's end, making it the perfect time to inject fun into your team's experience. Remember the power of the surprise birthday cake? It packs a punch because it's unexpected. Now's a good time to deliver a surprise to re-energize your team. Just like you, your team feels tired. Some probably even need help managing burnout after months of extra work. While you have done a lot of work to create space for a broader range of emotions—anger, frustration, and grief, to name a few—you also need to make space for positive emotions: appreciation, feeling valued, gratitude, curiosity, confidence, hope, joy . . . and even fun!

You can nudge toward fun by creating **closure rituals**. When done as a community, these moments honor memories and emotions of loss. This can help close a chapter while acknowledging the positive aspects of the past. For example, some standard shifts to emphasize during the sustainment phase are:

- "We let go of working in silos, and now we work as a team."
- "We let go of using paper to do our work. Now we have automated, routine tasks."
- "We let go of being order-takers, and now we have information to be strategic partners."

Each shift presents an opportunity to create a fun, joyful, and memorable experience. This is how you design the high end of the peak experience moment to help people remember the positive aspects of change. Amplifying positive emotions in whatever activities you design turns them into closure rituals and celebrations such as:

- A team-based scavenger hunt or ongoing trivia contest that symbolically blows up silos
- A controlled bonfire or shredding party for the old paper forms no longer in use
- A team lunch with business partners where they "take the orders" and recognize your team by serving the food

The joyful celebrations overtly and symbolically reinforce the benefits of the change. The "dip" in the emotional roller coaster typically lasts months, so balancing that with amplified celebrations and fun helps bring your team out of the funk. You are designing peak experience moments in your change and want the high point to be more memorable than the low point.

Celebrations also counteract negative memories of previous change efforts. Your team wants to feel good about their accomplishments, so design celebrations to help them feel the upside. The month following go-live and the first time you complete a crucial process (i.e., run a successful payroll, complete quarterly reports) are critical moments for a celebration. Even though you may be experiencing low energy right now, know that offering this gift to your team will help to re-energize them *and* you.

## Rewarding Change

You cannot overdo praise and encouragement during behavior change. Developing a comprehensive plan that consistently, frequently, and systematically rewards your team becomes your focus in the sustainment phase. Your rewarding change plan includes both formal activities that take a bit longer to implement, such as submitting team members for various recognitions and awards, promotions, and financial rewards; as well as informal activities, such as daily praise and encouragement or an invitation to a meeting that signals leveling up. Rewards happen through what you say and what you do.

Let's look at the Rewarding Change Model:

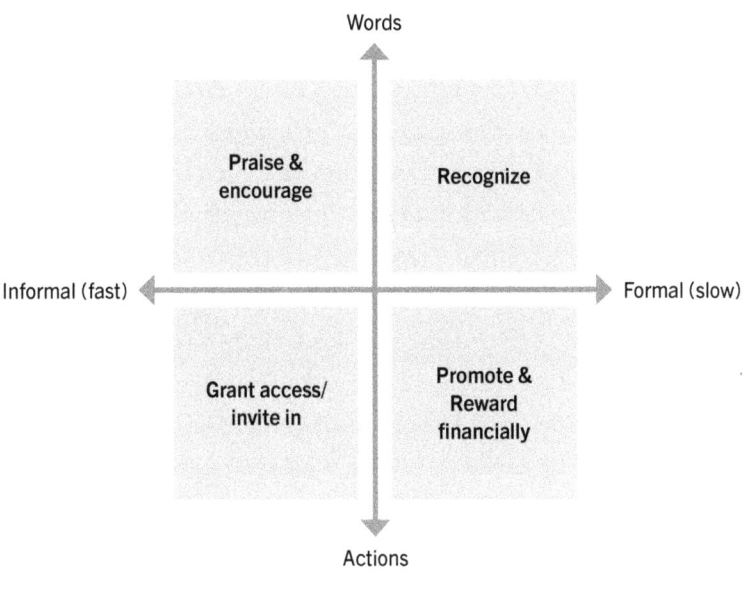

*Figure 6*

When using this model, start with the easiest and fastest way to make an impact: catch people trying to do things right every day, and praise them. You've already started this through positive nudges with individuals. Now you want to do a lot more of that to combat your team's frustration when they feel they aren't "good" at their evolving jobs yet. Encouragement makes them want to keep practicing.

According to psychologist and author Barbara Fredrickson, the magical ratio you are striving to hit is three to one. In other words, make sure you deliver a positive, encouraging message three times as often as you correct missteps. To operationalize this, consider how you regularly interact with your team daily and create habits to deliver positive messages. Dedicating time to walking around or checking in are the simplest ways to do this consistently.

Another fast way to reward change is to use access to leaders as a visible cue that team members have leveled up. This tactic can informally acknowledge key people, such as your business change lead. Being invited into a leadership meeting or having access to other influencers in your organization signals growth. Inviting someone into a trusted circle may be the most underutilized reward, yet it's so easy! Extend an invitation to key individuals to participate in leadership meetings or offer to introduce them to other leaders to share what they learned. These invitations can happen quickly and informally, well before you get approval for a formal promotion or title change.

More formal ways within your comprehensive rewarding change plan that take longer to implement include leveraging existing recognition programs within your organization. You may also nominate team members for formal awards within or outside your organization or ensure your entire project team receives recognition in visible employee programs. You can supplement existing formal recognition programs by creating a team-specific recognition to acknowledge contributions from team members over many months on top of day-to-day responsibilities. Many teams do this type of recognition monthly during team meetings throughout the project, or you can do it once at the end through a fun outing for the entire team to celebrate closure together. Better yet, do both!

Finally, formal actions to reward change that require more planning on your part include financial awards, title changes, and promotions. Financial awards can be both monetary or less tangibly, a benefit such as a bonus day of paid time off. Special consideration for formal financial rewards or promotions should be made for those who contributed more substantially to the project, such as your business change lead, your workstream leads, the system admin team, and potentially testers who participated significantly. Special one-time bonuses outside annual performance reviews or promotions during the year following a large project require you to start planning early to make a direct, visible connection between contributions to the project and the reward. Finding volunteers for the next change will be easier when people see the opportunities result in rewards and recognition.

## Rooting Out Resistance

The period immediately after a significant change launches also brings any remaining resistance to the forefront. You will see people who are adopting new behaviors and others who are lagging. Suppose you have done everything in your power to make the change easy, yet some people aren't doing the new behavior. Why? The two most common types of behavior non-compliance are:

1. **Learning laggards** who need more *skill* to do it and more training, guided support, and repetitions. You'll recognize these people as those who are trying

but need more time, practice, and perhaps different ways of learning.

2. **Saboteurs** who need more *will* to do it, as they are intentionally avoiding doing the behavior. This requires consequences. Instead of focusing on making the behavior easier, you find ways to make not doing it harder.

Both types of people do not perform the new behavior. The key is discerning why so that you can choose the appropriate remedy to address it.

In technology adoption, Joe Bohlen and George Beal documented in their article "The Diffusion Process" that laggards account for 16 percent of a group. This represents a small number of individuals, but you'll want to quickly determine why for each person, which is as simple as asking them directly. Here's such an example:

> **YOU:** "I noticed that you haven't logged in yet. Is there a reason why?"
>
> **ANSWER A:** "I forgot my password and got locked out. I need help." [Learning laggard, skill]
>
> **ANSWER B:** "I haven't had time." [Saboteur, will]

You can provide appropriate nudges after pinpointing whether it's an issue of skill or will. Learning laggards need more training support, while saboteurs need a consequence. Sometimes the question resolves the problem because the person knows you noticed. If resistance persists beyond a few nudges with your saboteurs, your actions resemble the steps usually taken to correct and improve performance issues.

You may want to cut team members some slack and give them more time to adopt new behaviors, such as extending the deadline to log in to the system. Not addressing it makes the change optional. Stick to your original expectations, particularly if your organization historically allows people to opt out of changes. You have clearly communicated an expectation about a behavior, so a direct corrective conversation is warranted to hold individuals accountable.

A second form of sabotage shows up more subtly. In rare cases, people look for loopholes or ways to avoid new processes and behaviors. Adopting a "criminal mind" means stepping outside your usual thinking. It's asking yourself, "If I didn't want to go along with this, how would I surreptitiously avoid doing it?"

One example that occurs frequently during system rollouts is when two different roles can approve a request. Suppose both the supervisor and HR can approve an employee's time-off request. A supervisor might avoid adopting the new behavior of approving requests by perpetually allowing HR to do it. As a result, they quietly avoid the new behavior and undermine the intent of the change for supervisors with direct knowledge of business needs to approve or decline time-off requests.

When designing the system, giving both roles access to completing the approval seemed like a good compromise because it represented a new responsibility for supervisors. But you just made it easy for supervisors to avoid changing their behavior. Remove HR as an approver, and make it impossible for supervisors to avoid doing it. Solutions to behavior noncompliance can be creative and nonconfrontational. The worst of what you allow will persist. Use the months following a change launch to achieve behavior adoption and root out resistance.

## Continuing Improvement

In the sustainment phase, you will simultaneously root out the resistance of saboteurs and listen to feedback from those on the other end of the spectrum who already have ideas about how "better" can be even better. Those team members who adopt and embrace change early will say things like:

- "I wish we had a report that could tell us how many..."
- "I would be more excited if we could..."
- "What if we tried changing..."

While it might feel like the team isn't ready to take on more change yet (or hasn't budgeted for it), the comments help direct how to talk about what's next. You can ask those who have improvement ideas to participate in road map planning (this is another example of an "invite in" to give access, since usually only a few leaders guide planning for what's next). More broadly, when you begin talking about the process for improving things, you send the message that the change is here to stay. You continue influencing your team's momentum until the "new" way becomes routine and behaviors are repeated consistently. Then the transition for this specific change is complete.

Yet while one change is completed, more change has already been added in virtually every organization. Thankfully, you've been building leadership behaviors shift-by-shift along the way so that you can apply them to more change. Every leader builds skills through consistently performing behaviors until each becomes an automatic habit.

Using the four quadrants of the Human-Centered Change Model from chapter 4 as a guide, you can gauge your current skills and where next to focus. With each level of performance improvement in your change leadership, you increase your capability to accelerate change adoption. The more you move toward holistic change leadership that includes managing tasks and leading people, the more likely it is that change doesn't disrupt your team or business. It simply becomes part of how you perform at the highest levels. Change isn't an event; rather, it becomes a way of working.

## Cera Day's Story

Cera Day breathes a sigh of relief as she exits the online discussion of her last weekly project meeting. She's glad to be done with this project! Except that she knows there's more to do to complete the transition with her team. She reflects on how, for the next year, each new cycle will bring learning with it. Rather than longing for work to return to normal, she sees the opportunity to continue building a high-performing team.

She switches gears to finish writing this week's thank-you notes, which she's done on personalized cards selected for the handful of individuals she wants to ensure feel her gratitude for their contributions to the team. She starts with a note to her business change lead:

*Dear Athena,*

*When we set out on this adventure a year ago, I could never have envisioned how much I would grow as a leader. You are one of the reasons for this. Your positivity and curiosity have been infectious! Time and time again, I observed you patiently answering questions and showing your colleagues how to complete tasks—many of them utterly foreign to you. You gathered feedback from your peers that helped me make better decisions and know when there was an issue and how I could help. It's also brought me joy to watch you grow through this experience. I'm immeasurably grateful!*

*— Cera*

Cera may be tired, but spending time recognizing her team gives her the energy boost to address the resistance she's observed in a few team members. She can recognize the difference between those who are slower to pick up on doing things in a new way and those who intentionally avoid doing what's required in their role. After the work that the team contributed to bringing this vision to life, she won't tolerate a lack of teamwork. Thankfully, it's only a couple of individuals, and brief yet direct conversations corrected each issue. She had to do a lot less correction than the effort she made to praise and encourage through regular rounds of observing her team working following go-live.

Overall, Cera is proud of how the team has navigated the past year's challenges. Some gained skills that make them natural fits for the next step in their careers. She's got several title changes that better reflect their new responsibilities, and even a couple of promotions are targeted for next year. She smiles as she thinks of how excited those deserving team members will feel when she rewards their contributions.

While the details remain fresh, Cera's also documenting individual contributions to make annual performance conversations more specific and meaningful. The entire team will receive a spot bonus approved by executive leadership, who also surprised Cera by serving lunch at a recent team celebration.

*Rewarding Change*

The team was proud to know that their work was appreciated at the highest levels of the organization. She hopes the combined rewards and recognition will help her team feel the depth of appreciation she has for their contributions.

Some of the team are so energized by this upgrade to their work tools that they're already discussing ideas for improving the system. Cera's channeling that enthusiasm into the enhancements exercise led by Sergio. Team members are looking ahead now that they've seen how things can go well. She knows that with the following change, some of her team members will immediately lean into it with optimism and excitement.

Cera would like to think she's helped make change positive rather than something to dread. It feels good to be on this side of change. Fear, frustration, and even grief have been part of the experience, but so has joy.

For Cera, it feels like an ending *and* a beginning.

*One Small Shift:*
## CELEBRATING GROWTH

The project plan tells you when the tasks to manage are officially done, but you know your work as a change leader focusing on people continues in perpetuity. So keep up with your nudges to influence behavior change, plenty of praise and encouragement, and supporting those who are ready for more. By this stage, you are celebrating growth—yours *and* the team's, including making memories together through fun. Bolstering the pleasant emotions involved in change cements you solidly as the influential, people-first leader your team wants to follow because you help them feel good.

Courage Is a Single Step:
Serving Others Is More
Important than Fear

# 10

# COURAGEOUS CHANGE LEADERSHIP

*Putting People First*

The email subject line catches Cera Day's attention: "Seeking advice." She doesn't recognize the name coming from outside her organization. Who is this? What does he want?

She opens the message and reads:

> Dear Ms. Day,
>
> I hope this message finds you well, and please forgive my directness. Your system implementation team gave me your name. We'll be using them for our upcoming implementation. They suggested I get in touch with you about learning from your project. Would you be willing to share your experiences over lunch? I would greatly appreciate hearing your perspective.
>
> Best regards,
>
> An Liu

Cera chuckles. She knows precisely how An feels; even his polite tone can't hide the fear behind this email. No doubt he's overwhelmed, with anxious thoughts racing through his head about everything that needs to get done—most of all, the people side and leading the team through it. *I've come a long way,* she reflects with gratitude. *Meeting with him will allow me to solidify everything I've learned.* She schedules the lunch.

The following week, Cera meets An at a quiet restaurant where they won't be interrupted.

"Thank you for meeting with me, Ms. Day," An greets her halfheartedly and seats himself hurriedly. His eyes give away his stress; Cera can see that he appears tired and is probably not sleeping well. Red flag number one: He's already not taking care of himself to make it through the marathon. Cera has become a quick study of people, thanks to all her practice over the past year in understanding emotions and observing behaviors.

"You're welcome," she says. "I'm more than happy to share our experiences. I know how hard it is. It's daunting to think about everything you've got to do early on. My mind bounced anxiously from one task to another, and everything felt like it had a steep learning curve."

"Yes, this change will challenge my team," An replies, deflecting the attention away from himself. Cera notices this and wonders if he realizes how important he is to his team. He goes on to say, "I'm honestly not sure they're up to it. So many of them aren't what I would describe as 'technical' or resilient. I'm not sure I've got the right people. I'm curious about your team and grateful to meet you in person. I've heard fantastic things about how smoothly your project ran. It was described as an example of how to lead change. Have you done this before?"

Cera laughs graciously while noticing that he's talking about his team as possible villains, not a joint heroic effort. "No, this was my first change leadership opportunity. I'm flattered to hear this feedback. But I'd be quick to say that there's no such thing as 'perfect' for projects or change. It's simply about staying invested in your people. There were many times I wanted to give up, and it felt terrifying and exasperating. I had no idea what to expect or do. There were surprises around every corner—far more than what I'm used to in my day-to-day role. It required me to stop micromanaging by trying to control everything. I became a better leader, and my relationships with my people reflect that."

Cera hopes she can bring the focus back to An and what's in his control: his leadership actions and why he's doing it—for his team.

"How did you become a better leader?" he asks. "I'm not sure what questions to ask, other than to have you tell me everything you know. I've never done anything like this."

"Well, you're already on the right track by asking for advice!" Cera encourages him, knowing he needs plenty of praise and specific tactics. "You'll need a network of people to support you, including peers outside your organization. I'm happy to give my perspective beyond just our lunch today. You'll also need a go-to person to help with change. Everyone on our project team grew from the experience, but our business change lead, Athena, grew the most.

"Athena was an invaluable partner. She had a better handle on the details of things, like training. Plus, she saw firsthand how her peers were engaging—or not—in requests like testing. She was my reality check for how I was doing as a leader, and she listened to the feedback that other team members weren't courageous enough to share directly with me.

"That's probably my number one advice for you: Get help from within your team, from peers outside of your organization, and from your system implementer. Our internal project manager worked alongside Athena and me. Together, it made the change more doable, as we each had our role to play. The panic I felt about trying to get everything done lessened once we put that team in place. It also felt better to me, as we could pick one another up when specific challenges got overwhelming. I'm so grateful for the relationships I built through this, which helped me grow into a better leader. I don't think our environment was perfect at the start, but a concerted effort to help everyone feel like they could speak up to share concerns and ask questions made a big difference to me becoming a better leader quickly through their feedback. Our team conversations became much more collaborative and solution-oriented, too."

"That's good advice because I certainly don't have time," An responds abruptly, quickly writing notes but failing to look up at Cera to make eye contact. He seems more concerned about the tasks.

Cera pauses before clarifying her statements. She doesn't know An well enough to ask more direct questions about his emotions, so she guesses he's as terrified as she was back at the starting line. He might not even be sure what "good" looks like.

Ironically, Cera knows that the skill that changed the most was her capability to observe emotions and use them to influence behaviors. She can notice which emotional category is present, and more granular forms of fear like anxiety and apprehension jump out to her more quickly now. She has more language for talking about emotions, too. The swirl of emotions involved in change doesn't overwhelm her anymore. If she's being true to herself, what she feared most wasn't the mountain of work but the emotions. She recognizes the emotional roller coaster for what it is to her now: a joyful ride!

It's hard to tell someone all the ways they'll grow when they're just starting. Sometimes the missteps are the best teachers. It's truly necessary to experience the challenging parts of the hero's journey of going from "good" to "bad" and then "better." Cera feels the upside now, but she can remember the lowest point, too, when her team was frustrated and sad.

Returning to An's statement, Cera has her tough love ready for him. She's not afraid to call out emotions before nudging into action if that's what the situation requires.

"Even when you're scared of not being good at it, you'll need to prioritize it to find the time," Cera says, noticing and naming An's fear and nudging him toward the best choice. An appears surprised by her directness but shows he wants to hear more by shifting his eyes from his notebook to meet her gaze and putting his pen down.

She continues, "Your role as a leader is serving as the coach on the sidelines who masters the playbook. But you are also the quarterback for some plays. Needing and getting help isn't about letting the game go on without you. It's about coordinating the various players you need so that the team succeeds. That's keeping a focus on the next first down, but you're the only one who sees the entirety of the game and the long-term goal. Not every play succeeds, and learning from that is vital."

"Ahh, I see what you're saying," An responds. "Regarding my role, it's more 'yes-and' instead of 'either-or.' I've got to do the big-picture stuff and some of the blocking and tackling."

"Exactly," Cera says. "You've got to roll up your sleeves for some of it so that your team sees you're in it with them, but not so much that you run yourself into the ground or others aren't getting a chance to learn, too. One of the things I needed to change about my management style was a tendency to control.

I learned I didn't have a people leadership skill set. There's a difference between getting all the tasks done and succeeding on the people side by building relationships. It's not possible to pin everything down. I learned to let go and delegate, which helped my team grow, and I think that has made me a better leader."

"You seem to have a natural way of talking about all this," An says. "Have you always been such a good storyteller and teacher?"

The compliment catches Cera off guard, and she smiles.

"I don't think my team would have described me that way a year ago," she says. "I was a good manager and kept tasks moving, but now I am a leader focused on inspiring, encouraging, and developing my people. They're the why that kept me motivated when things got hard. Funny enough, strengthening my relationships within and outside of my team brought a lot more joy into my work. There were even some fun moments along the way!

"I was intimidated by the people side and afraid of the messiness of emotions. But I grew so much in that regard. I recognize them without reacting now, and I appreciate the importance of using them to influence behaviors. Keeping my emotions in check not by withholding but by being calm created the right conditions. Our team started asking more questions and expressing concerns, and my calm helped me make better decisions. Being clear-headed allowed me to focus more on the ways I could help my team build confidence. I do a lot more encouragement now, too! That positive energy is infectious. Our whole team's demeanor has become more optimistic. Working together to accomplish a hard thing does that."

"Yeah," An says. "If I'm being honest with myself, I have much to learn about being OK with talking about emotions with my team. I don't have that capability. How did you do it? How did you do it all?"

Cera reads An's doubt. She knows mastering change leadership takes effort. This past year has been a career-changing growth opportunity for her. She's learned about good change leadership and gotten a chance to practice behaviors. Her mindset has shifted from a black-and-white perspective of "can" or "can't" into one of possibilities.

"Yet," she affirms. "You haven't mastered it *yet*. Early on, it feels like there's so much to learn, and most everything is outside your comfort zone. For me, that was hard because I was good at doing my job the old way. I could do it on autopilot. I could efficiently get the tasks done and manage the process, which made me feel confident. But I was also limited by that comfort.

"It was uncomfortable getting outside of that zone, but now there are more possibilities. I feel energized by challenges. Shifting my mindset has changed how I feel about work—and myself."

"It's certainly inspiring to hear you talk about it," An says. "A year feels like a long time, but I know it will go quickly. I don't feel ready."

"The next year will be full of things that will make you uncomfortable," Cera says. "It's OK! That discomfort is a sign you're growing. If you learn from each one, it'll get easier. Looking back, I don't think I could have done it without taking it one step at a time.

"Sometimes I felt petrified of making a mistake. But with a bit of practice in calming my nerves, I got better at figuring it out. When you slow everything down, you'll know. Or, at least you'll feel more ready to try something, which is always better than being stuck in fear."

"I admire your courage," An says.

"Becoming courageous happens one small step at a time," Cera says. "I feel fear all the time. But it's easier to keep going when I remember that I'm doing it to help my team. They make it worth it."

## *One Small Shift:*
## INSPIRING COURAGE

The natural tendency in times of uncertainty is to try to control the chaos. That looks like overreliance on the "managing tasks" side of the Human-Centered Change Model from chapter 4. But change requires the other side, too: leading people. It's change leadership that inspires, encourages, influences, and develops people that creates a lasting impact on teams. These leadership behaviors require a more developed understanding of how emotions influence behaviors.

Remember, how you *feel* influences what you *do*. Emotions can hinder progress toward goals, or they can be used as fuel to achieve visions. They can cloud judgment and impair collaboration, but they can equally inspire hope and open minds for problem-solving and learning.

Deeper emotional understanding starts with fear because that's the natural human reaction to new situations. Recognizing fear in the moment allows for a conscious response and a faster shift into productive behaviors. When leaders show their teams how to shift into possibilities despite fear, they help their team move forward. Through small steps, you can become a powerfully inspiring and influential change leader . . . and it all starts with fear.

# Bibliography

Barrett, Lisa Feldman. 2017. *How Emotions Are Made: The Secret Life of the Brain*. Boston: Houghton Mifflin Harcourt.

Beal, George M., and Joe M. Bohlen. 1956. "The Diffusion Process." *Increasing Understanding of Public Problems and Policies: 1956*: 111–121. doi:10.22004/ag.econ.17351.

Brown, Brené, 2018. *Dare to Lead: Brave Work. Tough Conversations. Whole Hearts*. New York: Random House.

Bridges, William, with Susan Bridges. 2019. *Transitions: Making Sense of Life's Changes*, 40th anniversary ed. Boston: De Capo Lifelong Books.

Cialdini, Robert B. 2021. *Influence, New and Expanded: The Psychology of Persuasion*. New York: Harper Business.

Clear, James. 2018. *Atomic Habits: An Easy & Proven Way to Build Good Habits & Break Bad Ones*. New York: Avery.

Chapman, Diana, Jim Dethmer and Kaley Warner Klemp. 2014. *The 15 Commitments of Conscious Leadership: A New Paradigm for Sustainable Success*. Self-published; Dethmer, Chapman & Klemp.

de Becker, Gavin. 1997. *The Gift of Fear: Survival Signals That Protect Us from Violence*. New York: Dell Publishing.

Edmondson, Amy C. 2018. *The Fearless Organization: Creating Psychological Safety in the Workplace for Learning, Innovation, and Growth*. Hoboken, NJ: Wiley.

# Bibliography

Fogg, BJ. 2019. *Tiny Habits: The Small Changes That Change Everything.* Boston: Houghton Mifflin Harcourt.

Fredrickson, Barbara L., PhD. 2009. *Positivity: Top-Notch Research Reveals the 3-to-1 Ratio That Will Change Your Life.* New York: Harmony.

Gilbert, Elizabeth. 2015. *Big Magic: Creative Living Beyond Fear.* New York: Riverhead Books.

Kornfield, Jack. 2008. *The Wise Heart: A Guide to the Universal Teachings of Buddhist Psychology.* New York: Random House.

McCauley, Cindy, PhD. 2022. "The 70-20-10 Rule for Leadership Development." Center for Creative Leadership (blog), April 24, 2022. https://www.ccl.org/articles/leading-effectively-articles/70-20-10-rule/. (NOTE: This is where you can learn more about Robert W. Eichinger and Michael Lombardo's 70-20-10 formula, which is referenced in chapter 8.)

Nhat Hanh, Thich. 2012. *Fear: Essential Wisdom for Getting Through the Storm.* New York: HarperOne.

Pink, Daniel H. 2009. *Drive: The Surprising Truth About What Motivates Us.* New York: Riverhead Books.

Psychological Safety, powered by Iterum. n.d. Accessed March 15, 2024.

Rendon, Jim. 2015. *Upside: The New Science of Post-Traumatic Growth.* New York: Touchstone.

Russell, J. A. 1980. "A Circumplex Model of Affect." *Journal of Personality and Social Psychology* 39, no. 6: 1161-1178. https://doi.org/10.1037/h0077714.

Seligman, Martin E.P. 2006. *Learned Optimism: How to Change Your Mind and Your Life.* New York: Vintage Books.

Taylor, Jill Bolte. 2021. *Whole Brain Living: The Anatomy of Choice and the Four Characters that Drive Our Life.* Carlsbad, CA: Hay House.

# Bibliography

Thaler, Richard H., and Cass R. Sunstein. 2021. *Nudge: Improving Decisions About Health, Wealth, and Happiness.* New York: Penguin Books.

van der Kolk, Bessel, M.D. 2014. *The Body Keeps the Score: Brain, Mind, and Body in the Healing of Trauma.* New York: Penguin Books.

Walker, Pete. 2013. *Complex PTSD: From Surviving to Thriving— A Guide and Map for Recovering from Childhood Trauma.* Self-published; Azure Coyote Publishing.

# Acknowledgments

I've dreamed of becoming an author since I was a child. The writing comes easily for me. It's the sharing part that's more challenging. I attribute my ability to publish this book and fulfill that childhood dream to the healing work that began in late 2020. Putting in the work with the help of professionals and support of empathetic friends has changed how I experience the world, and therefore, what I can contribute to it. I'd like to thank Chris Wheeler Doe, Dr. Dana Harrington, Andrea Iten, Jana Johnson, Sigrid Nielsen, Jen Noetzli and April Podhradsky for supporting my healing. Thank you for reminding me that I am human first. This book exists in the world because of you!

As for the craft of writing, I want to thank two mentors. My high school journalism teacher, Miriam Kagol, who nudged me towards studying journalism and my first "real-job" boss, Larry Haeg, who brought newsroom discipline into a corporate communications setting. Back then, we printed drafts, and I dreaded seeing red pen markups. Your judicious guidance tightened, clarified, and brought more punch to my writing. Thank you for teaching me to choose my words wisely. This book is shorter because of both of you.

As for the book creation process itself, I want to thank developmental editor Marisa Solís for shepherding me through

## Acknowledgments

concept formulation and content creation. She helped me get all the words out, including finding a way to tell the story with heart using Cera Day. Copyeditor Sara Letourneau whose meticulousness gave me peace of mind during the fine-tuning stage. Thank you both for helping me feel supported during the most vulnerable points—getting started and knowing when to call it done. For helping package it all beautifully, designer Rachel Valliere. Thank goodness for professionals who strive to honor the creative vision while executing details with precision.

I am also grateful for the beta readers who provided feedback to improve the manuscript: Gus Broman, Ed Cox, Becky Frayer, Melanie Hohertz, Sara Lobkovich, Karen McCarren, Sarah Moran and Elisabeth J. Trach. Thank you for persisting through the bumpy parts. You gave me perspective through the reader's eyes, which allowed me to amplify powerful points and eliminate distractions.

Finally, to my family. My parents, Paul and Linda Jennings, who nurtured my creativity and honor my sensitivity. And to my source of strength: my husband, Matt, and two delightful adult children, Alec and Avery. Thank you for listening, encouraging, and celebrating with me. The next one will be easier. I promise!

With deep gratitude,

Kris Jennings
August 2024

# Putting It Into Practice

*free mini-course and downloadable tool kit*

Reading this book will provide you with an understanding of core concepts, models, and techniques to lead organizational change. To help you put these ideas into practice, access the free mini-course that includes downloadable tools. Find more support here:

**https://www.krisjennings.com/Inspiredtoolkit**

www.ingramcontent.com/pod-product-compliance
Lightning Source LLC
Chambersburg PA
CBHW052129030426
42337CB00028B/5080